PATHWAY TO PROFITS

*A Mr. Biz Guide to Running Your
Business Like a Boss*

Ken "Mr. Biz" Wentworth

PATHWAY TO PROFITS
A Mr. Biz Guide to Running Your Business Like a Boss

© 2019 **Ken "Mr. Biz" Wentworth**

Published by: Mr. Biz Media
Columbus, Ohio

Cover design: Masoud Charkhkar

For author speaking inquiries, contact: Info@MrBizSolutions.com.

For discounts on bulk purchases, contact:
Info@MrBizSolutions.com

Contents

Acknowledgements

Thank you to my amazing wife, **Dusty**! There is no way I could have written this book without her unyielding & overwhelming support. She makes me a better person every day with her unintentional daily reminders (as a nurse) on what it truly means to be a "giver". And . . . she tolerates my crankiness during the book writing process.

Thank you to our girls, **Kylie, Emma & Kamryn**! They each inspire me in their own, unique ways and . . . they also tolerate my crankiness during the book writing process.

Thank you to my bro-ham, **Kevin**! He is always a good sounding board & pre-reader/editor. He has been an integral part of both books.

Thank you to my parents, **Keith & Patty**! Their example set the groundwork for the person I am today. They have always encouraged me to not set "limits" for anything.

Thank you to my "brothers from other mothers", **DJ Jeffries & Chris Elliott**! These guys have always given me limitless, positive support & are willing to help at the drop of a dime.

Finally, thank you to **Frank Kern**. I never, in a million years, planned on writing even _one_ book until he showed me how "easy" (wink-wink, nudge-nudge) it was. One cool dude who has indirectly helped me tremendously.

INTRODUCTION

My goal with this book is to give small business owners everywhere a simple blueprint for success! We all work so hard to achieve our dreams and I want to help you make them happen!

After my first book, Amazon best-seller – "How to Be a Cash Flow Pro" - it became increasingly apparent that I needed to help small business owners in a more profound way! Of course, cash flow is a critically important topic to cover but there is so much more.

That being said, I want to share more of the blessing I have been given with business owners everywhere! The Biz Family aren't the only ones who should have to hear all of the business knowledge bouncing around in my dome – haha! Just ask any of them – Mrs. Biz or our 3 daughters, who "tolerate" my business musings on a regular basis. I can't help it – it's just how I'm wired!

That being said, let's get real for a minute . . .

- Do you work too many hours?
- Are you happy with the money you make for the hours you work?
- Do cash flow struggles keep you awake at night?
- Does your business cause you to miss family events?
- Is getting your company to the "next level" a regular concern?
- Are you wondering how you can make "it" work?

If any (or all) of these points speak to you, this book will help you! No doubt – no questions asked!

This book covers **THE** topics that most often present challenges to small business owners. We surveyed small business owners worldwide to ensure we hit the topics that most often create challenges.

Here is what we cover in this book (in no particular order):

- How to minimize collections to maximize cash flow

- What to expect when you're financing

- How to get to the top of your vendor's "pay pile" each month

- Who wants more revenue? Anyone? Bueller? Ferris Bueller?

- Creating game-changing results with a budget

- Is your business as efficient as it should be?

- Hire better people faster!

- What external risks are lurking in your business?

- When **NOT** to DIY your business

- Managing vendors for better pricing & service

I purposely hit cash flow hard because that is what causes 82% of small business failures[1] and is the problem I most often encounter with my clients?

Due to a compelling response, I have purposely broken this book into two volumes. The aforementioned topics are all covered in this book. However, due to the small business survey, we are already planning a "Volume II" of this book.

You are likely thinking – why not just cover everything in one book, Mr. Biz? Well . . . that's a great question!

As a small business owner myself, I know I regularly struggle with time as a constraint. I constantly wrestle with finding time to continue learning while also balancing running my business and spending time with my family. What small business owner doesn't face that challenge?

Who has time to read a ~400 page book? I know if I saw a book that long (even if I thought it could help me), I would likely skip it.

---

[1] https://www.nfib.com/content/resources/start-a-business/why-do-small-businesses-fail/

That is precisely why I decided to break "Turning Problems into Profits" into two separate, much more manageable, ~200 page volumes. We can cover these critical topics more comprehensively and make each more easily consumable.

I hope you find some outstanding information in this volume that helps you move your business forward.

To keep apprised of the 2nd volume, as well as TONS of free content, be sure to connect with me on social media.

Facebook: Mr. Biz Solutions

LinkedIn: Ken "Mr. Biz" Wentworth

Instagram: MrBizSolutions

Twitter: MrBizTweets

We will offer discounts for Volume II to those that purchased Volume I, so be sure to connect with us!

MrBizSolutions.com

SECTION ONE

CREATING FINANCIAL EXCELLENCE

Chapter 1

LET'S GROW SOME REVENUE!

Now we're going to talk about a topic I'm sure everyone is keen to hear about and that is, "How to increase your revenue." If you break it down, in its simplest form, there are really only four ways to increase your revenue:

1) Increase your number of customers

Let's talk about this one in a bit.

2) Increase the average transaction amount

To accomplish this, you up-sell. A good example of this would be: McDonalds. You visit McDonalds and order a cheeseburger – what happens? They ask the question that became ubiquitous in pop culture a while back – "You want fries with that?" And more often than not, they'll also follow that up with something like, "For only 25 cents more, you can add a drink."

That's an up-sell; *that's* increasing the transaction size. Otherwise, without up-selling, they would have only made $2 for one cheeseburger. With the benefits of up-selling, they've successfully turned that one $2 cheeseburger into a $5 meal. That's a 150% increase in revenue from just two, simple questions. If the patron declines, no harm-no foul. All good.

Now, consider how many times that scenario plays out in every single McDonalds, every single day. What impact do those two simple (upsell) questions have on their annual revenue? Holy schnikeys!! Absolute genius from a business perspective!

Let me frame that for you – you won't believe these numbers:

McDonalds is a bit stingy with their stats but consider this[2] –

- Customers served <u>daily</u> – **69 million**
- Hamburgers served per <u>minute</u> - **75**
- Fries served <u>daily</u> – **9 million lbs**
- Big Macs served <u>annually</u> – **550 million**

MIND. BLOWN.

Now, consider those volumes when contemplating the impact of the previously outlined up-sell scenario! Absolutely astounding!

When discussing revenue growth, of course, we cannot leave out another behemoth – Amazon! I'm sure most people reading this have ordered something from Amazon at some point or another. During your purchase, have you ever noticed, when you're ready to check out, there's always… ALWAYS a few pictures

---

[2] https://expandedramblings.com/index.php/mcdonalds-statistics/

and links showing that "like-minded" people who bought this product, also bought these products… Right?! Extra things there that you may be interested in and, of course, potentially buy. That's another example of an up-sell strategy. I must confess – probably 1/3 of the time I've seen those suggestions, I've at least seriously considered buying one of the complementary products, so it's definitely effective.

How about you? Have you ever/how many times have you made additional purchases from Amazon's suggestions?

3) Increase the frequency of transactions per customer

This can be done in many different forms. One form is to utilize cross-selling. So, ultimately, you're selling *other* products that you have to your current customers.

Another way is to introduce or offer a product the customer needs to purchase on a regular basis – for example, vitamins. They buy a month's worth of vitamins and need another month's worth the next month and so on. Sell products that necessitate *recurring* orders.

4) And then, of course, the most straight-forward method to increase revenue is to simply increase your prices

I'm going to save elaborating on that one for last, because there's not a whole lot, frankly, to talk about with that. Although, I am going to give you some tips on things to look for when you are increasing your prices to help ensure you don't get yourself into a bad situation. We don't want you to increase your prices to the point where it's detrimental to your business, which is a risk.

We are going to go through these four different ways to increase your revenue. That said, I want to talk first, in detail, about how you can increase the number of customers you have. I'm sure it's something that *everyone always* looks to do.

The first thing to do depends on what your business is. Of course, not all of these suggestions will work for all businesses. However, no matter what your business is, you can almost certainly seek to extend your market area. Depending on what type of service you offer, you should have a solid understanding of how you can branch out from the vicinity in which you're currently working.

If you have a service business, such as: plumbing, HVAC, electrician, landscaping, etc., there are several key factors to consider. Chief among those would be:

- Additional mileage on your vehicles – what is the cost associated with that?

- Additional travel time for your technicians – this will "cost" your business money as well because travel time is non-revenue generating time!

There are definitely things to consider with geographical expansion. When it comes to the price of your services, we need to make sure that it's effective *and* profitable for you and still a good value for your customers.

Another way to increase your number of customers – and this is an easy one – yet is one I think a lot of people miss – is to:

Create referral or affiliate partnerships

Find businesses that are complementary to yours, and partner with them. This will allow you to refer business between each other and/or you can work out an agreement where you're giving them some type of referral fee. In order to ensure the referral is profitable, rather than a flat fee, you can consider providing a percentage of the revenue they refer to you.

Another way to increase your customer base with referral partners is with affiliate relationships. If you are unfamiliar, it is where other people outside of your company promote your business and you compensate them with a predetermined formula. It could be flat fee; it could be a percentage of the revenue they generate for you. Finally, of course, it might be a combination of both.

This a bit different than just a straight referral because, oftentimes, your affiliate partners actually pay out of their own pocket to promote your business. There are people who are affiliate partners with several different businesses and that is what they do for a living! They literally just promote other businesses and collect their fees.

We know it works when done well – it's common in the online community and has been all the rage for the last ~15 years. It works especially well for online businesses because the entire process can be automated on both ends. Your affiliates get their own links to your online products, then when someone they refer buys, their commission is automatically calculated and paid out.

A business with a massive amount of affiliate partners is ClickFunnels.

Russell Brunson has it figured out and dialed in like a boss

He has an entire army of affiliates pushing his products each & every day 24/7! Of course, this is in addition to his company's internal marketing efforts. ClickFunnels affiliates can even earn cars and I'm not talking about rusted out '78 Pintos! How much business are they sending to ClickFunnels to earn a car (on top of their normal commission)??

On a smaller scale, the affiliate world is also alive and well amongst Amazon sellers. I mention that to emphasize that affiliate relationships can work for businesses large and small.

However, before jumping into the affiliate world, you need to consider the potential downfalls. Specifically, you have no control over how your products are marketed & displayed to the marketplace. Unfortunately, your affiliates might not share your same ethical position.

Read into that what you will but just be mindful of it

The next option with increasing the number of customers you have is, as those of you who listen to my radio show (B2B Radio) know, you can always increase your marketing spend. The critical premise of that is you have to make sure you're doing things effectively. By doing so, you'll be getting an acceptable return on your marketing spend.

The guidance I recommend on marketing spend is you should spend between 2% and 15% of your annual revenue. Even in dire times, you should strive to stay at or above that 2%

threshold. Of course, if you're in tough times, your revenue is likely down so that 2% is a lower number.

Typically, you will want to be in the 2-8% of revenue range

The 9-15% range would typically be utilized for specific opportunities and usually for short periods of time. For example, you might be in startup mode and re-investing income back into the business to grow it more quickly. You might be managing a campaign to promote a new product or location. You could be trying to gain market share on competitors. Those are a few examples of when it might make sense to spend at the top of that range.

With that being said, you need to make sure that you can measure what you're getting from each of your marketing avenues. Admittedly, sometimes that can be difficult to do, but it is critical you do so to ensure what you're doing is profitable. Determine your baseline to make sure that you're getting a 3x, or 300% return. For example, if you're spending $10,000 on marketing, you should expect $30,000 of revenue from that $10,000 spend.

Next, another one I really like and I think is under-utilized –

Create a sales contest during your slow season

If you are the sole salesperson in your company, you can still make this work by morphing it into increased offers or sales during your slow season.

When your down season arrives, instead of just relinquishing yourself to the fact you're going to have slow sales and a dip in revenue, create a sales contest for your sales people and have a prize at the end for the winner. Post updated results every week to keep everyone focused and energized.

Jazz it up a little – if your prize is a vacation, include some props/pictures of the exotic location – get creative to motivate them! We did this at one company and the prize was a cruise. At each week's Monday morning sales meeting, the owner would share results and include, "Tips to Get on the Ship". On the results page each week, the admin would include a picture of the contest leader's head photo-shopped onto someone having fun in the sun. It was hilarious and everyone looked forward to it. Everyone wanted their head super-imposed on that week's image. The reveal each week had a powerful impact on each & every person included in the contest.

Note: To be effective, run it during the *entirety* of your slow season. This will really get those guys and girls working hard during that slow season to ensure they're not just settling for slow times. By doing this only during your slow season, you provide a balance so neither they nor you allow it to be something that you just 'get used to'. It will also keep your employees motivated with a healthy competition.

Another way to increase the number of customers you have? If you don't have one already, you **have** to set up an online store.

I know some people are calling for the death of the website. I am not one of those people (not anytime soon anyway). I still recommend that almost all businesses have a website to showcase the products and services you offer. It's the perfect way for you to point someone in your direction. Let's put it this way – what is one of the first things you do when you need a service or need to buy a product and you don't already have a vendor in mind? Do you Google the product or service? I know I do!

What if someone recommends a company or you see/hear an advertisement from a new business? Do you just instantly call them and make an appointment or buy from them? Or, do you look them up online? Let's suppose the latter, which, by the way, is the vast majority of consumers . . . if you find they don't have a website, what do you think? Often, if you don't have a website, people perceive that you're not really a serious business, or that you might be a little "fly-by-night" type of operation. Obviously, that's *not* the portrayal you want in the marketplace.

Further, when you don't have an online store, you are neglecting a potential huge advantage over your competitors. According to recent research, e-commerce is growing 23% annually[3]. Think about that – over a ~4 year period, sales are doubling up!

Here a few more statistics to consider[4]:

- 75% of Americans have purchased something online

- 63% of Americans who have bought something from Amazon

- 63% of Americans = 92% of all online shoppers

---

[3] https://www.statista.com/statistics/288487/forecast-of-global-b2c-e-commerce-growt/

[4] https://smallbusiness.com/ecommerce/online-shopping-statistics/

So, generally speaking, of folks who shop regularly, people are now more comfortable making purchases online. And, by the way, do you think that percentage is likely to grow or subside? The millennial generation has grown up with online shopping being the norm. Heck, I'm not a millennial, but both Mr. & Mrs. Biz prefer online shopping! Future generations will only continue to exacerbate that online impact. Do not miss that opportunity!

Think about this – at this point even the basic necessities, groceries & the like can be ordered online to be delivered right to your home! Don't be naïve to think this won't become the norm as we move forward.

If you don't have an online store, you are potentially missing out on all of that, already vast & rapidly growing, market! If you think that number isn't going to continue to increase into the future, I've got some swampland in Florida I want to sell you. ☺ Personally, I can tell you my family is part of the online majority.

How about you? Do you prefer online shopping vs. in-person shopping? Personally, I'd much rather go online and have a bigger selection, rather than driving around to five different stores trying to find what I'm looking for, only to find that they're out of it! It's just a more efficient use of time. As you know, Mr. Biz is all about efficiency.

Considering those stats, did you know that:

Only 54% of small businesses actually have a website[5]

---

[5] https://www.thebalancesmb.com/reasons-small-business-website-2948414

Think about that... almost half of small businesses do not have a website. I think that's crazy! I don't care what kind of business you have, I think you need to have a website, even if it's a simple website, for the reasons I mentioned earlier.

Taking this a step further and closer to generating revenue:

Only 26% of small businesses have an online store[6]

Wow – talk about a huge opportunity! Flip the script – on average, 74% of your competitors do not have an online store. The market is wide open. The market that **prefers** to shop online, no less! Think of how much potential revenue that could mean for you. And before you tell me that you run a service business and this doesn't apply to you – not so fast, my friend! Let's say you are a plumber – what are some of the most common items homeowners need from you? Sell those! How about selling a maintenance plan online? You can send existing customers to your website for that. Let customers pay for your services in your online store. That will improve your cash flow and get you out of the collection business. The list of opportunities goes on and on.

The other element an online store possibly adds is convenience for your customers. I'll give you a quick example:

I was working with a specialist medical practice. Of course, as a medical specialist, there are certain products they have that their patients need on a regular basis and many wear-out. For example, as an orthotic practice, you might have a boot on your foot or ankle; a brace on your knee or specific orthotics for your

---

[6] https://www.webmarketingpros.com/study-shows-74-of-us-small-business-dont-have-e-commerce/

shoes. Some of those products need to be replaced and there is a convenience factor for your customers when you make these items available on your website. If, like in this case, your patients can easily go online and order it and have it delivered right to their house, they're likely to replace them on-time, as needed.

Think of the alternative – they have to make an appointment at the doctor's office, which could be a pain in the neck *and* it could be 2-3 weeks before they can get an appointment. If you're trying to fit it into your work schedule, *when* can you get away from work to get to the doctors just for them to look at you and say, "Oh yeah, here you go" with the new product. Or, even just trying to stop by the doctor's office, which often has the typical 9AM-5PM schedule – what if you also work during those hours? Chances are, if you're the patient, you're going to put off replacing whatever item it is you need, thereby decreasing the frequency of your purchases and decreasing revenue.

If you're the doctor or medical supply company, you may lose the sale altogether, because they may buy the product while they're running other errands over the weekend (when you aren't open). It is all about time & convenience for people. Time equals convenience. You have to make it easy for people to do business with you.

In order to offer patients that convenience factor, we opened an online store and guess what . . . it absolutely *exploded!* We began including the online store information on discharge papers when people would leave the office. We told them about the store and how they could easily use it get what they needed without having to come into the office. They could just order and have it delivered directly to their house *without* having to take time off from work. Patients absolutely loved it! It took off and revenue from it went through the roof vs. the previous onsite product sales.

There is a whole litany of things you can do with your website. I don't want to get too far off topic here, but while we're talking about creating an online store, I want to mention a few things. One being to check the speed of your website and compare to what it should be because speed is a significant factor when people buy online.

We have almost become A.D.H.D. If it takes too long, we get distracted or quit all together. You don't want to lose out on sales just because your site is slow. That is usually a simple fix for a web person so please don't neglect it.

Think about it… if you click on a webpage and it takes five seconds to load the page, which doesn't sound like a lot of time, but that's practically an eternity for a website, right? We're used to things just 'popping up' right away. Hence, the need to check the speed. If that is outside of your comfort zone, hire someone who's well versed on that topic.

Along the lines of website optimization . . .

Work on optimizing the meta titles on your site. Simply put, they are one way search engines find pages on your website. They are brief descriptions of each page. Many people neglect them and miss out on this free way to help your site rank better. Most people can handle DIYing it on this topic. You can do a quick search and find instructions on how to make this happen.

On the paid side, you can work with Google and their AdWords advertising. Also, you can look at the 'conversion versus visitors' calculation. This will reveal how many people visit your site for a given period. You can see how many pages on your site they visit, how long they stay on each page; heck, you can even install a heatmap to see where they spend their viewing time on each page. This might also indicate where you lose them. If it is consistently in one spot on the page, you can edit that content to make it more visitor-friendly. Then, and more importantly for revenue growth, you can see what percentage of them *actually* buy from you.

Along the same lines, another one of those typical things to measure… the abandoned cart. This reflects when people put an item in an online shopping cart but leave without buying. You'll want to 'retarget' those people because they are obviously very interested in your product. Maybe something happened – for example, they lost their connection or didn't have the time to enter payment information; maybe they were in the middle of checking out on their phone & got interrupted by a phone call?

Almost 40% of all e-commerce purchases in the 2018 holiday season were made on a smartphone[7]

Another possible reason for an abandoned cart – you require customers to register on your site. 14% of people will abandon

[7] https://www.outerboxdesign.com/web-design-articles/mobile-ecommerce-statistics

the order if you require them to register[8]! Don't worry though – there is an easy fix. Just use the "continue" button and you can still get basic info from them. Obviously, they have to give you their email address, and their mailing address for you to be able to mail them their purchase. Boom – problem solved!

 Now, let's move into that second piece we talked about at the outset – increasing the average transaction. In other words, the up-sell of the McDonald's fries I mentioned – the "Do you want fries with that?" question; the Amazon, "You know people also bought this product" suggestive selling technique.

I want to mention one thing before we continue. Something I think that sounds obvious when you say it out loud, but gets overlooked too often – don't forget about your current customers! I'm not talking necessarily about retention. I'm talking about targeting some of your current customers because you might offer products they may need or may be able to use. However, they may not even know you offer that product.

This will vary by business *and* by industry but according to a recent small business survey stated that:

65% of new small business revenue comes from *existing* customers[9]

The point being: don't forget to market to *them!* We're always seeking to obtain new customers but we miss the fact that we already have a captive audience of people who *already* like us. If you view new purchases on a 5-point scale, your existing

---

[8] https://www.wordstream.com/blog/ws/2016/03/17/shopping-cart-abandonment
[9] https://smallbiztrends.com/2016/10/customer-retention-statistics.html

customers are already 4/5 of the way there! You have already cleared a bunch of hurdles with them:

- They know who you are;

- They know the quality of your products;

- They know they can trust you.

Since you've already cleared a bunch of those hurdles, now it's just a matter of offering another product that would be beneficial to them. So, remember to market to current customers! This will increase the frequency of their purchases and potentially increase their average transaction size.

Another way to increase your average sale amount is to:

Bundle your products

You can do this on the service side *and* on the product side. For example, if you are a pet groomer, you're offering a service, but may also be able to create an opportunity to sell them pet products, such as: brushes, toys, shampoo or food.

Now that you know these things, you will see them in many different forms and in all kinds of businesses. Keep your eyes and ears open and you will see it everywhere! That, in itself, is a clear indication that it works. It creates a sense of value and convenience, as well. If you're able to bundle purchases together vs. buying things individually, it's usually cheaper and a lot more convenient! Instead of paying $10 each for four products and it costing $40, you may sell those four products together for

$35. That's a $5 savings for your customer and it also increased the perceived value for them.

An example – everyone talks about bundling services for your entertainment – think internet, TV channels, movies, cell plans, etc. When they bundle those services, they get additional revenue out of you and get a little deeper into your pocket. On the other hand, you save money so that's *definitely* something I recommend on both ends.

Another strategy that inspires increasing your average transaction size is referred to as a "tiered sale."

Let me explain: What I mean by that is (and you've definitely experienced it before as a consumer), the more you spend, the bigger the discount you get. For example, they might offer $10 off your first $100 spent. Then, you get $25 off $200, and so on. Usually, the discounts increase. In that example, you're getting 10% off the first $100 you spend, then you're getting 12.5% in the example of $25 off $200. That tiered sale tactic is *definitely* effective. Think for a second how many times you have encountered it yourself.

Here is another illustration of how a tiered sale can be powerful

Using the prior offer example, if a customer has $170 in their basket and they're getting ready check out – they may say to themselves (or maybe your cashier points it out) – "Gosh, if I spent $30 more, I get an extra $15 off!" They start to do the math in their head to justify spending more to save more, right? "If I spend $30 more than I was already going to spend, I'm going to get an extra $15 discount (because at $200 they get $25 off vs.

only $10 for $100). I'm really getting 50% off my last $30!" In many cases, they go look for $30 of additional spend to increase their discount from $10 to $25.

An important point to consider with offering discounts, sales, etc.: either be a business that rarely offers discounts or one that offers discounts often. I would be hesitant to be the latter. Let me explain why . . .

I'll use the example for people that are familiar with Kohls Department Stores. You *never* buy anything at Kohls for regular price because they run sales promotions *all* the time! When I say all the time, I mean all the time! If you pay regular price for anything at Kohls, you're either desperate or you're not a wise consumer.

In addition to weekly sales, they regularly have promotions where they issue their "Kohls Cash". Kohls Cash is credit towards a future Kohls purchase during a specific upcoming timeframe. However, even though you are saving, they get you back into their store (or online). By regularly offering these types of sales, you are creating a finicky customer base. They may get to the point where they say, "Gosh, I'm not going to buy from 'so-and-so' because I know they're going to have a sale soon. I'm going to wait until the sale to buy." First, you create an environment where you have to offer a promotion to get sales. Also, while your customer is waiting for your sale, they may purchase from another merchant and you lose the sale altogether! Point being – don't overdo it.

Another variation of a tiered sale is to change the way you determine shipping charges. When you have to ship products, you can offer something similar to what Amazon does. For example, you can offer free shipping for orders greater than a certain dollar amount. How many people out there (I would say raise your hand, but I'll never see it) have experienced this?

You go to buy something from Amazon and you see that you're only $6 short of free shipping and shipping is going to cost you $8 or $10. In that situation, what are you going to do? More than likely, you're going to go find $6 worth of stuff to buy so you can score free shipping!

And actually, it might not end up being only $6 because you can't find many items for exactly $6. So, you actually go *over* the original threshold, but you do it and feel good about it because you saved that shipping charge. Speaking for myself, I've justified it in my head to say, "Well, that was kind of like… free." In reality, of course, it's not *really* free. This will show you how powerful this is: 40% of people will add things to their cart to reach that threshold while shopping on Amazon. That means that 40% of the time, when you have that "free shipping" threshold, you're going to get a larger transaction size!

If you want to give this strategy a shot, you have to make sure that you really, *really* dig into the pricing. If you don't, you'll only get yourself into trouble. Even Amazon doesn't offer free shipping on everything. For example, if you have something that is awkward, heavy or just plain expensive to ship for whatever reason, you probably want to make sure that product is not eligible for free shipping. In doing so, make it *very* transparent on your website so you don't end up with angry customers who put items in their cart all the while expecting free shipping, then find out that item is not free to ship and they abandon the cart.

They might be ticked off enough to never shop with you again. Or, even worse, they vent their frustrations on social media –

OUCH! Not good

A viable (and simpler) alternative to 'free shipping' is to offer *discounted* shipping at different spending thresholds. While it isn't as enticing as "free shipping", you can implement in much the same way you would a tiered sale. The more your customer spends, the higher their shipping discount. This strategy also eliminates the need to exclude certain products from a 'free shipping' offer. Of course, as always, you need to run the numbers and incorporate this into your pricing model to ensure the offer is incremental to your earnings. As with 'free shipping', if you skip this step, it could be quite detrimental to your overall earnings.

It could slyly disguise itself as Fool's Gold – statistics show it **will** increase your revenue. However, don't fall victim to only focusing on the higher revenue. If, for example, your normal net profit margin (the % of revenue you keep after all expenses – different than gross margin, which only incorporates COGS expenses; these are often confused) is 10%, but you are generating incremental revenue with your discounted shipping strategy at a 3% profit margin, you are actually hurting your business. You are working much harder with the higher sales volume, but for less net profits. This scenario will inevitably lead to employee burnout and sleepless nights for the owner. The former typically results in employee turnover and the latter to extreme frustration –

"Our revenue has increased but we are making less money?!

What the heck is going on?! This just doesn't make sense!"

Unfortunately, I have seen this more times than I care to admit. Pricing impacts cash flow and cash flow causes 82% of all business failures. Even if your company survives, ignoring pricing and cash flow will have exacted an unnecessary toll on your mental health. There is absolutely no need for that!

Finally, in regards to up-sells, don't ignore the option of moving customers to higher priced options. I'm not, by any means, suggesting to arbitrarily to do this in a nefarious manner. However, if you offer a more robust product or service that might better fit your customer's needs, don't hesitate to present it to them.

You have probably seen national retailers do this but, perhaps, in a less-than-legit manner. For example, during Black Friday when they are fiercely competing for business, they advertise **THE** hot product of that season for a ridiculous price. Let's say it is normally a $300 product and they offer it for $50. Ignoring the Black Friday shopping shenanigans for a minute (oy vey!), you make your way into the store and find out – surprise! – they are all out of that $50 version . . . BUT they just happen to have plenty of stock of the $250 version (slightly discounted from normal).

Well, heck, while you have already gotten up super-early, maybe braved the weather, stood in line, battled with tons of people to make it into the store . . . what do you do? Statistics show that, more often than not, you will buy the $250 product because that was something you set out to buy that day. Going home without one would be a failure and, after all, it is still cheaper than normal, right? That is likely a version of bait-and-switch.

Another tactic looks like this – you see a deeply discounted price for a product. Once you get to the store, the salesperson tells you how awful that "cheap" version is. **BUT** . . . *this* product (right next to it or on the End Cap) is *so* much better! Here are the superior features you get with it – blah, blah, blah. And, oh, by the way, this version is more expensive, but still less expensive than you would expect.

Now that I alerted you to those goofy tactics, you will be on the lookout for them – sorry. ☺

I am not suggesting you approach up-sells from either of those angles . . . at all. I'm just opening your eyes to tactics used by other retailers, maybe even your competitors. Always do the right thing. Every time. No matter what. Use the Golden Rule – treat people the way you want to be treated. A mentor of mine says – treat the customer the same as you would treat your grandmother. I think both will serve you well in business and in your personal life. The world would be a better place if we all subscribed to those philosophies.

Now, if you will please give me a few seconds to jump off my soapbox . . . DOH!

You can utilize up-sells by presenting your customers with options to ensure they have a full picture of what you offer – from a product or service level. You might have three different levels for a particular product. **Honestly** present the merits and pitfalls of all three and let your customer decide. Same situation with services –

- you get 'abc' with level 1 for a cost of $x;
- you get 'mno' with level 2 for a cost of $y; and
- you get 'xyz' with level 3 for a cost of $z.

What you are likely to find is most customers will choose the middle option. Research suggests to either offer one option or three options. With three, people will predominantly choose option 2 because it seems to present the best value. I call it the Goldilocks theory – this one is 'too cheap' (level 1); this one is too expensive (level 3); this one is just right (level 2). There will always be outliers but option 2 will be chosen most often.

Going back to my original point . . . what if you only presented one option to your customer? They may have felt restricted – "this costs too much" or "this is cheap; it must not be very good" – and declined to buy because it just didn't feel right. Presenting all options enables your customer to make the best decision for them, which is ultimately what we want.

Another strategy to increase revenue is that of adding *complementary* products. One way to do that is to use the feedback you already have. When you started your business, you may have had an idea of the scope of things you wanted to offer. However, many of you will relate to this – feedback morphed your business into what it is today – good & bad, right? You'll always get feedback from your customers – whether you want it (and you should), or not – so you need to listen to it!

For example, if you're a restaurant owner – let's say a pizza shop – and you only offer pizza. But customers often say to you, "Gosh, my kids don't like pizza." Yes, that's an odd one because what kid *doesn't* like pizza but for example's sake, let's go with it. You may be getting requests for more "kid-friendly" items on the menu. If you get that request often enough, that's an opportunity for complementary products! If you currently don't offer other kid-friendly food and you have a sit-down restaurant, even if the parents like your pizza, at best, they're going to order takeout. And, it's very likely they're not going to come in as often because in order to satisfy their kids, they will need to stop at a 2nd place for their food on takeout nights. You're going to lose that sale of kid's food, but also the pizza the adults already like. Then, they're not likely to dine in – hence, you may lose even more revenue from items such as, salads and soda and/or alcoholic beverages. DOH – fountain drinks & alcoholic beverages are likely the highest profit margin products you have!

You miss a *huge* opportunity because they're either not coming in at all or they're just ordering takeout. In this case, not offering that complementary product that might prompt them to dine-in. That's a simple example but definitely one that fits the bill for any business. Always listen to your customer feedback – what they're looking for, what they're asking for, etc. Doing so gives you a little more peace of mind when you're contemplating adding a new product. If you already know that your existing customer base has asked for it, you know there is demand to support adding it. As a result, you will be less likely to view it as a big risk. You're not taking a big chance because you *know* there's demand for that product, based on feedback, and it's an easy way to increase your average transaction size with your *existing* customers.

OK – let's move to the 3rd option for boosting your revenue –

Increasing the frequency of transactions per customer

There are many different ways to make that happen. As I talk through these, please keep in mind that some crossover into what we've already talked about, which makes them, I guess you could say, a underline double threat. These are good things and could help in both areas – average transaction size and increasing frequency of transactions.

To increase frequency, you should consider offering rebates. I remember, as a kid, companies seemed to offer rebates more often than they do now. My parents were always filling out some sort of rebate form – sending it in and waiting 6-8 weeks to get their ~$4 back.

A surprising statistic on rebates . . . redemptions on mail-in rebates are estimated to be only 60%[10]. Can you believe that? Sometimes people choose your product or service based on the rebate, yet 40% don't successfully redeem the rebate! That's a definite business 'win' because it keeps the cost of the rebate down for you.

And, get this one –

Rebates make consumers 75.4% more likely to make a purchase[11]!

Rebates are powerful!

---

[10] https://pocketsense.com/much-money-goes-unclaimed-mailin-rebates-9935.html

[11] https://www.dcrstrategies.com/20-rebate-statistics/

Rebates definitely help you increase your sales by increasing the frequency of your sales, which is exactly what we're talking about here. The fact that they only get redeemed 60% of the time lowers the costs of offering the rebate. It's essentially a discount – but it's not like giving someone a discount up front because they have to complete the redemption and they don't always do that.

The simplest example I can give you is if someone walks up to the cash register and you offer them an "on the spot" 10% discount. That costs you 10%... right then-right there. However, if you offer them a 10% rebate, stats show it costs you much less than 10%, right? On average, it's going to cost you ~6% because only 60% will redeem it. That is one way to increase your frequency of sales while also keeping your costs to a reasonable level.

I will say this – consumer sentiment towards a discount at the cash register is definitely more favorable than a rebate, but rebates don't fall far too behind overall. They can have a solid impact on sales. The other thing rebates encourage is repeat business because you're going to offer it on your products. It's not just they get $10 cash back.

Here is another way to increase revenue by increasing frequency . . . It's similar to a store credit in the form of a gift card. For your customer to redeem it, they have to come *back* into your store – in person or online. This also helps to build loyalty. It gives you *another* opportunity to continue to earn their business and build loyalty that is critical for long-term success.

Let's say, for example, they earned a $10 rebate for when they come back in the store. Are they going to spend $10? I mean, if it's me, I'm going to try like heck to spend $10 on the dot! But the reality is, they may not be able to do that. So, they're going to visit you again and likely spend more than just the $10 of the rebate, maybe $25. Now what you've done is two-fold:

1) You've earned an extra $15 ($25 spent - $10 rebate) of revenue that you may not have without the rebate

2) Besides the additional revenue, it spurs customer loyalty by bringing them back and also gives you *another* opportunity to make them a satisfied customer; you get that customer in the habit of looking to you for their purchasing needs

I'll give you an example using a restaurant, and this is a powerful one:

Typically, most people think that if you own a restaurant, you just need to get people in the door. While that *is* important to build brand loyalty, the measuring stick here is to have numbers to back it up.

Here are the facts, roughly as presented by Jon Taffer, long-time host of "Bar Rescue", during an interview with Gary Vee (Vaynerchuk):

When someone comes into your restaurant and they have a flawless experience, there is only a 40% chance they will come back to your restaurant a 2nd time. Even if they had good service and good food – only a 40% chance you get them back a 2nd time. That is much lower than I was expecting and shoots the commonly-held food service axiom of "just get them in the door once & treat them well".

Let's say they do return for a 2nd visit and have another flawless experience. What is the likelihood of a 3rd visit? Are you ready for this? You won't believe this – I know I didn't. It's only fair to inform you – despite your best efforts, you still have <50% chance of them coming back for a 3rd visit – about 42% to be more precise. Say what??

However, here is the line of demarcation you have been waiting for – if you can get them back for a 3rd visit – now your chances for them to come to your restaurant again (4th visit & beyond) are >70%. Finally, paydirt – YES!!!

The point of the matter here is you want to make sure you get people back in on a *regular basis*. As we were discussing (increasing frequency), how can we make that happen? You don't want someone coming in just once or twice, especially with a restaurant – you want to make sure you get them in at least three times so you need a plan to make that happen.

Heck, how do you get them in the *first* time? You can easily create a marketing plan to get someone in the door the first time. Lots of options there so I won't address them. If you work in that industry, you probably have better ideas than me! Create specials during different days of the week (tons of ideas/opportunities there), feature your signature dishes (the extra yummy ones so they love it and, not only come back, but also bring others to try it!), give lunch discounts to local businesses that are within walking distance . . . the list goes on and on. Make it happen!

The question remains (I haven't forgotten about you, restaurant owners!) - How do you get restaurant visitors back into your place three times to create that long-term loyalty?

The server asks every table (unless, of course, the guests are recognized) – "Is this your first time visiting us?" The first time they come in (let's assume it's a sit-down restaurant) you have the manager visit when they're finishing up their meal and getting their bill. Suppose this is an Italian restaurant:

<u>Manager</u>: "Hey, I see you had the pizza, how was it?

<u>Patron</u>: "Oh, it was great!"

<u>Manager</u>: "That's awesome. I'll tell you what – you have to try my Stromboli! We are known for our Stromboli – it's fantastic!"

The manager pulls out a business card, flips it over and writes: *'$5 Stromboli'* and puts their initials on the card. This is a critical point – not a pre-printed card and not from the server; a hand-written note from the manager – that shows importance. This makes your customer 'an insider', a VIP. That makes it much more likely they will return for their next visit.

Picture this: they are bragging to their co-workers or family – "Yeah, the food was great and the manager personally invited me back **and** gave me a signed discount card!" That equates to a high likelihood they will be back for another visit.

<u>Manager</u>: "Look, the next time you come in, give your server this card. Order the Stromboli & tell them I gave you this card."

When they return . . .

Server: "Thank you for coming back! You get your Stromboli for $5; Great deal – it's normally $10!" (This enhances the 'VIP' aspect; you're getting a great deal because you're an insider)

You're working towards that magical 3rd visit & increasing the frequency of transactions, while also giving your customer good value. You've gotten them back in a 2nd time and they're likely not going to come back to just get the Stromboli. More than likely, at a minimum, they're going to get a drink or maybe a salad. Further, based on the previous "brag factor", they're probably not going to come in by themselves.

In that instance, you're giving them the Stromboli at cost but they've brought another person with them or two, or three or four people. Heck, maybe they brought the whole family along? That all equates to additional revenue you would not have earned otherwise. Along with our 3-visit goal, more importantly, you've gotten them in for the *second* visit!

The manager and staff know it is their 2nd visit because they have the personally-signed business card on their table. Using that business card as a key indicator . . .

Manager: "Oh, man – how was everything?"

Again, your manager can judge this; feel it out a little bit; hopefully, they go over & see leftover boxes, which indicates two things:

1) They are full, and

2) The food was good enough that they want to take leftovers with them

Patron (hopefully): "It was great!" (If not, ask why it wasn't so you can learn how to improve)

Manager: "I see you already have boxes so I presume you don't have room for dessert. Is that correct?"

Patron: "Yes, it was great, but we are full!"

Manager: "I'm happy to hear you had a great experience. I'll tell you what – you **have** to try our cheesecake. Let me give you a card so you can enjoy free cheesecake."

Like before, you pull out a business card and write something like this on the back:

"Free cheesecake"

Of course, it isn't full-proof; it's not going to work 100% of time, but that is one way to get people into your restaurant three times! Give it a shot and let me know your results.

In keeping with our goal right now, you're increasing the frequency of transactions. Most importantly for restaurant owners, you've gained a loyal customer that you have a >70% chance will come back to your restaurant again. As you can imagine, beyond that 3rd visit, the percentages escalate exponentially. That 3rd visit is the magical unicorn!

Now, another one of my favorites for increasing frequency transactions, and this is a huge one – I encourage *any* business, no matter what type of business you have, to do this –

Create a loyalty/membership plan

Think along the lines of a wine club. Another example is candle of the month, beer of the month, etc.

I can "hear" the sighs of my service business readers already. In fact, I could even "hear" your eye-rolls! Really, people?! Haha. Do **NOT** skip to the next section or chapter. Have you not learned yet to trust Mr. Biz? I've got your back!

For my service industry owners, think about a monthly or frequent-user service plan. Let's say you're an HVAC company. Consider an annual maintenance-type plan, which is a form of a membership plan. Maybe $299 per year for a check-up in the spring & winter, preferred service, when needed, then 10% off any needed services? You can provide flexible billing – billed once annually or billed monthly, which includes a slight surcharge on the annual amount. Of course, as always, you would need to "run the numbers" to ensure the offer pricing is profitable.

Especially with HVAC, most people want to be able to "set-it-and-forget it". They don't want to worry about remembering to schedule appointments for their system. They just want it to work when they need it. Of course, as most know, the best way to ensure it "works when you need it to work" is to perform regular maintenance and that is where your maintenance program comes into play.

As with previously mentioned options, it is a win-win. You garner additional revenue but, more importantly, your customer wins in the long-run because their system always works! Or, if it doesn't, they get preferred service at a discounted rate. Further, you create customer loyalty so when it is time to replace their system, they are very likely to purchase from you.

If you're a bar/sports bar, I strongly consider promotions such as a Monday Night Football group (due to legal issues, you probably cannot call it that; no worries – Tip: create a name that is short/catchy, alliterative & incorporates your name – think, "Monday Nights at Marty's"), where customers get a ticket every time they come in on a Monday night for a football game. Maybe they can purchase drinks and some form of food at a discounted rate for their fee to be part of the group?

At the end of the season, everyone enters their tickets for weekly attendance. Those tickets are entered into a drawing for various prizes. Without much effort, you can secure sponsors to pay for (or mostly pay for) the prizes. Essentially, it doesn't cost you much, if anything.

In the bar/restaurant industry, Mondays are typically dead. So, for 17 of 52 weeks of the year, you're going to draw a bunch of new traffic on a typically dead night! More ideas – run specials when local teams play to increase the draw. Great situation there.

Create a community – maybe they need to be part of "the club" to be eligible for prizes each week? Wear your favorite team's jersey for 10% off your bill? Make people want to be there to watch the game. Have halftime trivia each week and award prizes. You can't win halftime prizes if you're not in the club. The prizes can be a combination of the host's branded materials and/or sponsor's donations (likely their branded swag).

Since, in the bar/restaurant world, Tuesdays are also typically slow days, give club members a discount on Tuesdays as well. It may not amount to much but it could increase business on an otherwise slow night. Maybe with the club discount (for example, maybe ½ off an appetizer?) they decide to bring their family in for dinner 3-4 Tuesday nights during football season? Who knows? It earns you recurring revenue, which is exactly what we are trying to achieve.

OK – with all due respect to my food service readers, let's shift gears. Let's talk about yet another way to increase the number of transactions per customer and this one can be internally influenced. In a nutshell, change the way you incentivize your salespeople. Wow – thanks for that stroke of genius, Mr. Biz. That sounds simple enough but, what do you mean? How can that increase transaction frequency?

Using a simple example – in a typical commission plan, salespeople might earn a 10% commission on the first $10,000 they sell. Then, from $10,001 to $20,000, they receive 5%; then beyond $20,001, they receive 2.5%. Presuming the upper limits are achieved & a 10% profit margin, illustrated as follows:

Sales	Commission	Biz Profit	Comm/Profit
$10k	$1,000	$1,000	100%
$20k	$500	$2,000	75%
$100k	$2,000	$10,000	35%

Put another way – if a salesperson sells $10k of product, they earn an equal amount to the company's net profit; if they sell $20k of product, they earn 75% of the company's overall net profit; at $100k of sales, the salesperson only earns 35% of the overall profit. That quite a difference and some of that differential is expected. However, consider, if you will, a different model.

Change it – flip it around – again, you need to run the numbers on this, but change it so that the more they sell, the more they get.

It depends on your product and how much it costs, obviously. You can't make it something they can never possibly attain. So, $0-10,000, we almost expect them to do that. So, maybe they earn 2.5% for that. But, when they get above $10,000, it goes to 3.5%. The point is, their commission is progressive! As they continue to bring in more sales, their efforts are increasingly profitable for them and the business. Why not share some of that with them to further motivate & incent them? That way they continue to push-push-push to get to that next threshold that jumps up significantly – right into their paycheck. The thing about most commission structures – if not done properly, they can be a little counterintuitive.

Most importantly, you have to ensure you're personalizing your customer service. Why do people leave? Why do we lose customers? Well, I'll tell you – 70% of the time customers leave because of customer service[12], **not** prices. Prices are a minority reason that we lose them. I cannot emphasize it enough – pricing is not the issue; it's a customer service issue. Obviously, good customer service is *very* important for retention.

A couple subtle, yet simple things you can do to improve your customer's experience. People love to hear their own name. When they visit and you've learned their name, make sure you use it! That makes them feel appreciated. Even if you don't know their name, if they pay with a credit card, make note of it and address them at that time by name:

"Mr. (or Mrs.) Jones" etc.

As mentioned, people love hearing their name; it has a *huge* positive impact. When people call in and you're doing any sort of verification of their account, or answering their questions, you already know who they are – use their name!

"Thanks for calling us, Mr. Jones. We appreciate your business" etc. People like that stuff, and it sets you apart from your competitors who *don't* do that. That customer may have called somewhere else, and that bar is low because the other company hasn't done that and you've done it

---

[12] http://www.customerexperienceinsight.com/the-no-1-reason-why-customers-stay-or-leave/

It pushes you to the top. Even in emails, don't address them with, "Dear Sir/Madam" unless, of course, you don't know their name. You want to make sure you put names in there, once you do know them.

Another classic example of how to improve this – if you send an e-mail out and at the bottom it says, "Do not reply to this e-mail address. It is unmonitored." You know how off-putting that is?! People hate that! Honestly, I don't like it either! Make it easy to do business with you. Not being able to just reply to an email is not making it easy to do business with you.

One final way to potentially increase transactions per customer – you can offer exclusive sales to personalize that customer's experience – maybe a coupon for their birthday, invitation to a few "VIP" sales during your slow season? In the long run, it will help with retention for that customer. A lot of it comes down to the what they call, "The rule of reciprocity." Easy for me to say, right? When you help someone and they know you're helping them, they almost feel obligated to help you back. That earns you more referrals and word-of-mouth advertising.

Another tactic that is very powerful – sending handwritten notes. Everyone loves a hand-written, personalized note. Of course, if you do a solid amount of volume, those notes can take quite a bit of time to create. Perhaps you implement a 'rule' that for any sale:

- > A certain amount automatically gets triggered for a handwritten note

- < A certain amount = no note; a simple verbal 'thank you' at the time of the transaction

- > A certain amount = personal note from the salesperson

- > A certain amount = personal note from the owner

I hope these revenue-generating tips have been helpful! As outlined, there are four ways to increase revenue. It is my hope you can utilize many of these methods to bring more revenue in the door.

As mentioned, please do not simply resort to increasing your prices. While that can be effective at times, it isn't always a profitable option.

Chapter 2

BUDGETING DRIVES GROWTH!

We're going to talk through the overall structure of budgeting and some reasonable approaches you can implement to create phenomenal results!

Let's get started; First, we'll start by defining budgeting. I think a lot of people think of it as almost a dirty word – most people don't like talking about budgeting. It's really just a plan. It's a roadmap for your business. People should be more afraid of NOT having a budget, than the budget itself.

For most people, I think the words "budget" & "diet" are met with the same trepidation. However, just like a diet doesn't have to be eating lettuce & drinking water at every meal, a budget doesn't have to be restrictive.

Without a budget is like flying blind. How do you make financial decisions? Do you have the money for *this*? Do you *not* have the money for this? For example, you think you need to hire a new salesperson. Well, does that make sense financially?

You can't just go on gut feeling. From a cost perspective, are they going to bring in enough money to support the additional expense? What if you need an admin position filled? That is an example of some of the issues and concerns that we will talk about.

That's one of the reasons why this so important – financial decision making. I've got a client currently that hasn't previously had a budget, so when it comes time for financial decisions, it's a contentious conversation. They want to invest in the business, but do they have the money for it? We don't know because they don't know their numbers because they don't have a budget.

You can budget not only your P&L, but you can also budget your balance sheet, which is another dirty word – the 'b' word – that a lot of people don't like to talk about… their balance sheet. If you have one, then you know your cash flow; what you can and can't afford.

There are a couple of different budgeting approaches. There are actually several but there are two that I'll focus on that are the primary ones. There's "zero-based budgeting" and then, there's what I'll call "incremental budgeting." Zero-based budgeting is essentially where you start your budgeting process every year with a blank sheet of paper and you justify everything. You start from scratch to build your revenue and you do the same thing on the expense side. You don't assume *anything*. You *literally* start from scratch and build from ground zero to complete your budget, and that makes a lot of sense for some businesses.

I think the more prevalent approach is incremental budgeting, which is using your prior results (actuals or budget from the prior year(s)) and build from that going forward. Using that, for example, we know that we had $1 million in revenue last year. We would then, using last year's numbers, aspire to have revenue growth of 10%. So, to put it simply, we're going project $1.1 million in revenue ($1 million * 1.10). Then, you go through your expenses in much the same way.

You go right down the line of all your expenses and make a decision for each line:

- Should it increase or decrease from the prior year?
- Will you give pay increases to existing staff?
- Do you need to hire additional resources?
  - How much will they cost?
  - What the timing of when you expect to hire them?
- Have employee benefit expenses increased?
- Will raw materials be more expensive?
- Do you want to spend more money on discretionary things, such as marketing, advertising, etc.?
- The list goes on and on – you review each line

If you have a prior budget or know what you did the prior year, the incremental system is a reasonable approach. It is less time consuming as well. However – beware of getting caught in this common predicament – this is the way we've always done it. Don't get stuck in that sort of thinking and not really justifying well enough, *all* of your expenses and how you're spending your money. It's easy for us to get lulled into a sense of complacency. You have to really guard against that and make sure you're not falling into that state of mediocrity.

And then, of course, budget timing comes in many different forms, right? You can create a budget on a quarterly basis. You could do it semi-annually. However, the most common budgeting timing approach is fiscal year budgeting, or a full 12 months. 95% of businesses use January through December as their fiscal year.

The approach I prefer and the one I'd like you to utilize is to start with a 12-month budget, and then adjust that as you go along through the year. For example, you re-evaluate your budget after you have April results and then again once you have August results. I refer to that as a "forecast." You could also view it as budget version 2.0 and budget version 3.0 for that year.

That isn't to say you completely scrap your budget and just re-forecast your way out of shortcomings. Quite the contrary! I typically use the re-forecasts as an opportunity to raise the bar higher. Consider this scenario: thru April you are running ahead of your budgeted $1.1 million annual revenue by $100k – you are kicking some serious butt! That means, on average, so far this year thru April, you are running $25k per month ahead of revenue. Projecting that same $25k per month run-rate would equate to exceeding your annual budget by $300k! In that scenario, I would push to re-forecast our annual revenue to $1.4 million (original $1.1 million + $300k).

If the script is flipped and we are behind budget, I don't lower the budget. Oh no, my friend! I will increase May-December numbers so we still can meet our original $1.1 million annual budget. This clearly shows us what numbers we need to hit each remaining month in order to still hit our original annual revenue goal. Essentially what you're doing, is using your history *and* your current environment to project the future.

Let's dive into budgeting for revenue. You'll hear executives in business use the terminology, "the top line", which is your revenue. You definitely want to start there. Start with your sales goals for the year. If you're a company that has several different sales folks, determine what their individual sales goals are, then project what type of revenue you're expecting to derive from each of their contributions.

A couple of things to keep in mind for revenue:

1) You want to make sure you're considering all of your revenue streams, not just *exploring* your different revenue streams. If you're going to introduce anything new during the year, such as services or products, you will need to consider those factors when creating your budget.

2) Make sure you consider any "fixed" revenue you may already have in place, such as subscriptions of some sort. You may have a service you provide to which people subscribe. For example, if you sell widgets, and you know how many widgets you can project based on subscriptions, project what you're going to sell and implement it into your "top line".

There are a ton of things that go into projecting revenue. As I mentioned previously, using history and the current environment to project your future requires considering the local economy, the national economy, the global economy, the interest rate environment set by the Federal Reserve (in the United States), etc. You have to ask yourself, "How will these interest rates and the current economy impact *my* business?"

Another one of the things I'll mention is if you have the ability to do so and you're considering adding to your marketing/advertising budget, you're going to be reinvesting in your business. What you "reinvest" varies widely.

I recommend investing 2-15% percent of your revenue for this particular piece. Based on your net revenue, you would expand your business if you choose to spend on marketing or advertising. And again, it varies widely, for several different reasons, as you can imagine. However, if you're in a heavy growth mode, and maybe you have a new product coming out that you really want to push, then you're going to get closer to that 15% threshold while you emphasize that new product.

Another thing to consider is maybe one of your competitors has left the market, or for whatever reason, you really want to grow your market share. If a competitor has met their demise, do not hesitate to push the thrusters down and capture their market share via additional marketing. However, that scenario is typically rare and, even if applicable, it is short-term. Hit it hard for a short period of time to capture those customers, then be done.

If things are already tight and you need to tighten things up even more, you would obviously lean toward the lower end of the spectrum. So, the reason I mentioned that, from a revenue budgeting perspective is that anytime you invest in marketing or advertising, it's an expense you wouldn't necessarily think of to tie back to your revenue. I'll focus on that because it's an important part to consider when creating your budget.

You should expect to get at least a 3x return on your marketing/advertising investment. What I mean by that is, let's say you're spending $10,000 a year on marketing, that should equate to at least $30,000 in revenue. And if you suddenly say – "I'm going to increase that to $20,000". That $20,000 should reap at least $60,000 in additional revenue. Obviously, more is better, but it should be at least 3x your spend.

If it's not, you need to change your marketing or hire new marketer because they're not effectively marketing your brand.

When you create your revenue budget, if you're going to increase your marketing/advertising, you should anticipate that impact and implement it into your budgeting plan. That's one of things I think people miss often.

Most importantly, you're tracking against this budget *every* month to ensure you are on track and moving forward with realistic and attainable goals. Make sure you're reviewing that with your sales people. Maybe you're the only salesperson right now, but every month you're checking in to see where you are. Depending on if you have cyclicality in your business, you want to appropriately spread that goal out – not just in a straight line. Straight-lining is easy but, in most cases, not even remotely effective.

What I mean by that is – to make it simple – if your goal for the year is $1.2 million in sales, and you say, "Well, I'm just going to straight line it – we should have $100,00 per month in sales." That's not necessarily how it works though...right?

Depending on what your product is, let's say you sell ice cream. If you live in a climate that is seasonal, obviously you're not going to sell as much ice cream in December as you do in July. In Ohio, for example, where you know you've got summertime temperatures that will generate more ice cream sales, you have to ensure your revenue budget reflects that seasonality.

If you just straight line it, you're going to think you're behind in January, February, and March; when you're expecting $100,000 in each of those cold & slow months. But, in actuality, you'll catch up throughout the year, generating the most revenue in the summer months. In this case, you may only make $40,000 in May, but bring in $160,000 in June, hence creating an average of $100,000 per month for those two particular months. While the months individually would look crazy, when combined they meet your annual goal of $100k per month. Of course, there are 10 other months we need to consider but these two are on-point.

As outlined, you'll want to add some cyclicality/seasonality into the formula. That's when you can use the history of the business and see what your typical sales have been throughout the year, first quarter, second quarter, third quarter etc., to make sure you're adding that seasonality in an accurate manner. These are just some of the different approaches to take on your revenue. That being said, including seasonality is critically important! Without it, you can't be sure how you are trending.

Consider this scenario for further illustration:

If you ignore seasonality with your $1.2 million annual goal, you will project a monthly revenue goal of $100k. However, what if you run a northern business that is dependent upon the weather? Something such as a lawn care company. Most northern climate lawn care companies make the bulk of their revenues in the April through September timeframe. So, January through March are SLOW months. Without including cyclicality in your budget, at the end of March you would expect to have $300k in revenue ($1.2 million / 12 months = 100k per month). However, you have $0 in revenue! You would be ready to jump off the nearest tall building because you are $300k behind! That scenario does not account for the seasonality in your business.

On the flip side, what if your business made the majority of its revenue in the winter months?

Let's say through the end of March you have accumulated $450k of revenue. If you just use the straight-line method, you will be popping champagne bottles because you will think you are 50% ahead of budget:

> Straight-line budget through March = $300k of revenue
>
> Actual revenue = $450k
>
> $150k above a $300k budget = 50% on the plus side!

However, as Lee Corso says on College Gameday – "Not so fast, my friend!"

In this scenario, you are about to head into several months with no revenue. Let's say April through October don't amount to any revenue. Put another way – you need to earn all of your $1.2 million in annual revenue during November-March. That's just 5 months! While this is a bit of an extreme example, these types of cyclical scenarios do exist. Depending on your industry, it may even be prevalent.

Almost all businesses have an element of seasonality/cyclicality.

Don't miss that when budgeting!

Next, on the expense side, you can budget expenses in a few different ways. You can look at your discretionary vs. non-discretionary expenses. Or, you can consider fixed vs. variable. The latter is probably the more likely scenario and how people most often look at things.

For fixed expenses such as: rent/mortgage, utilities, debt service on your assets, insurance, etc. You know those are all things that are fixed expenses. Obviously, they can vary significantly with each business. The goal is always to limit fixed expenses. Optimally, we want 100% of our expenses to be variable. That way, our expenses change in direct correlation to our revenue. Wouldn't that be utopia?!

I'll put it this way – if you can create a business that is 100% variable AND the margin is positive (that is KEY!), you will be a gazillionaire in no time because you can quickly scale it without regard to expense.

If 100% of our expenses were variable, our expenses would move in lock-step with our revenue. For example, if our expenses were 80% of our revenue (that would mean a 20% profit margin), we would know that for every $100 of revenue, without fail, we would have $80 of expense and therefore $20 of profit. If that was the case, we could scale our business like crazy because we would know for every $100 we invest, we would receive $20 of net profit. While that doesn't sound like a lot on the surface, consider if we scaled our business . . . $1 million in revenue would mean $200k of net profit ($1 million - $800 thousand of expense = $200k net profit). $5 million would mean $1 million in net profit, etc.

If only it were that simple!

Unfortunately, fixed expenses are almost always part of the picture. Think of your personal finances – you likely have a mortgage or monthly rent, maybe a car payment (or multiple), perhaps insurance for your dwelling or those vehicles, etc.

Typically, the way you would look at that is your variable expenses are driven by your sales. So, for example, your raw materials; if you sell 10,000 widgets, there's going to be much more raw material used than if you only sell 1,000 widgets.

Your marketing is variable (depending on how much you want to spend), and if you vary that (based on what we talked about earlier) to a certain percentage of your revenue. As you look at it (spending between 2-15%), if you're spending 5% and your revenues are up significantly, you will increase your raw dollar marketing spend.

However, if you keep your spend as a % of your revenue, it IS a variable expense – you spend more or less, dependent upon your revenue intake. You just need to ensure you stick to that variable formula. Don't just spend $x every month; stick to making it a % of total revenue to make it variable, which is what we want.

Here is another expense issue to consider:

- When should I hire a salesperson?
- Do they bring a book of business with them?
- How soon can you expect them to hit the ground

running?

- What type of sales numbers can you expect from them in the first 90 days, 6 months, 12 months, etc.?

Depending on when you bring them onboard, you need to allow for that ramp up time etc. Then, obviously, you're going to have expenses associated with them. Having a budget is a way to determine that and keep an eye on it to make sure it makes sense when you want to expand and bring someone new onboard, whether it's a salesperson you might be hiring or an admin person. Oftentimes, the owner wears a lot of different hats, and many of those hats end up being administrative in nature, usually because they may have started the business by themselves, or with only a couple of people. They're doing a lot of those admin functions as the business continues to grow and their other responsibilities grow as well. If this is you, you may need to give up some of those admin responsibilities.

One way to look at this if you're bringing on an admin resource:

What and whose functions are they taking over? If it's yours as the owner, what are you going to spend that time on? Needless to say, if you're bringing someone onboard and they're going to do 20 hours a week of admin work, that is going to free up 20 hours of *your* time. If so, what will you do with those 20 hours? Again, this goes back to the budgeting – if you're bringing those people on, then you're going to be freed up to spend that time doing business development or, hopefully, sales work. Therefore, you should expect more sales. Make sure you connect all of those inter-workings so they are accurately reflected in your budget.

Go back on the revenue side and think – "Hey, I'm bringing an admin resource on and I should expect more revenue!" Of course, that is counterintuitive – an admin resource equals more revenue?? That's why I'm mentioning it. Bringing on an admin person would increase revenue? Well, it should in this scenario, right? It will free you up to do more sales type activity and you should expect that. Make no mistake, that's the way for an admin role to pay for itself.

The other thing to do, and I've mentioned this previously – when you're not sure, bring someone in on a part-time basis. There are many companies that will allow you to have, for example, a virtual assistant – where you can pay them on a variable basis. Until you get to a point where a full-time resource makes sense, and the cost makes sense, hire them on a virtual and part-time basis! Only pay for what you need and use! Just ease them into filling that admin role; as your business expands, give them more hours. At some point as you grow, it will make sense to hire a full-time employee. Until then, use a virtual assistant.

Of course, with a virtual assistant you will pay a higher hourly rate vs. a full-time employee. But, keep in mind – you won't be directly paying any employee benefits and, if your resource isn't a good fit, you just make a quick phone call to garner a new resource! You don't have to re-post the job on your preferred platform; you don't have to schedule interviews; you don't have to choose a candidate and hope they work out.

Budgeting 101: scratching the surface here, but number one, on the revenue side – set stretch revenue goals. Stretch yourself and track against them every month of the year.

On the on the flip side, the expense side, I would look at it and say... always add a little bit of cushion for your expenses. You always spend more than you think. "Stuff" always happens, as they say. However, don't just add to every expense line. I prefer to keep each line lean & mean but add that cushion in a "Miscellaneous" line by itself.

Share the budget with your employees and consider profit sharing. When I say that, a lot of people cringe. You can set aside a certain percentage of your profits, even say 5%, and share that with critical employees. You need to know they'll help manage the expenses of the company more like their own, because in a sense, it is their own. This another topic we will dig deeper into in the 2nd volume of this book.

For more information on budgeting, go to www.MrBizSolutions.com. We have an online program that correlates with this book as well as proprietary budgeting tools for revenue and expense that I am certain will be helpful for you.

Chapter 3

GETTING TO THE TOP OF THE "PAY PILE"

In this chapter, we're going to talk about operational changes you can make to improve your cash flow by ensuring you get your invoices to the top of the "pay pile". Although it sounds almost the same, I don't mean "PayPal" . . . Pay. Pile. ☺

First of all – before we talk about the "pay pile" – let me start with payroll. With small businesses, especially if you're in any type of service business, payroll is typically your largest expense. It could be 70-80% of your expenses! If you're in manufacturing and you produce widgets, then probably not. However, it can be that much so you can imagine if you can impact 70-80% of your expenses in a positive way, it's going to have a huge positive impact on your cash flow.

Regarding payroll, I'll give you two tips on how to do that. The first is instituting a two-week delay on your payroll pay date. When you first implement this, your existing employees might not be overjoyed. You will have to work through those specific issues and maybe it's something you can't actually do. If you have a lot of employees that are living paycheck-to-paycheck (like most small businesses), you may have to come up with a gradual conversion into this.

However, once you have it set up and it's running smoothly, it only impacts new employees. It allows you enough time to invoice and get paid, hopefully, before you have to actually process payroll and pay for labor. It also provides more time to process payroll so hopefully you can eliminate or, at least, sharply reduce payroll errors. As you know, correcting payroll errors is time consuming and often costly.

If you think about it, t's fairly typical when you start a new job that you wouldn't get paid right away. This two-week delay for new employees should be easy to implement. It's the existing pool of employees where it becomes a little bit of a challenge.

The next tip on payroll is a little bit of an adjustment up-front for existing employees – if you pay bi-weekly, move to semi-monthly payroll runs.

For example, pay on the 15th and the last day of the month. This will have a positive impact because if you do bi-weekly payroll, there will be a couple months a year where you're going to have to fund 3 payrolls in one month – ouch!

You can imagine if payroll is 70-80% of your expenses, how much of an impact that's going to be when you have to absorb 3 of those in any given month as opposed to just 2. Putting this into place will go a long way to smooth out your expenses. And, frankly, it's going to help your employees in the long run because they will know they're going to get paid twice a month, not sometimes twice and sometimes thrice (What? Yes, I just said "thrice"). It will make it much easier for them to budget and plan for their personal expenses.

The second operational piece I want to mention deals with credit cards. So, two pieces to that . . .

Number 1 is, I would strongly recommend you obtain a business credit card. Choose one that has the highest rewards for the spending categories you will use the most. If you don't have one primary category for which you can take advantage, you can still find a card that offers at least 2% cash back. Be careful to read the fine print to determine if there are any spending caps on the rewards you can earn.

Be certain you consider that when comparing cards

Use your business credit card for all business-related expenses. Now, don't go crazy and spend a bunch of money you cannot afford to pay off when the balance is due! You have to keep an eye on that because I don't want you to carry a balance. I want you to be able to pay that off every month. Credit card interest rates (other than introductory periods) typically are much more expensive than getting a loan or a line-of-credit. If you need to carry a balance, consider one of those options vs. a credit card.

Having a business credit card has a ton of different benefits. One of which is most credit card companies will provide you with a summary of your expenses at the end of the year or at any particular time you may need it. This gives you a great summary of where your money is going. You can monitor your spending and the trends that go along with it.

For example, what did you spend on marketing vs. prior years? You can really do a lot of analytics around it. It's an easy way to track those types of things without you having to be a "spreadsheet jockey" (tip of the cap to a former boss, Craig Harrison, who coined that phrase). How many of us have time to do that on our own? Allow your business credit card company to do that for you.

If you do have a business credit card and you're carrying a balance on it, put your money towards paying that balance first since it is likely your most expensive debt. That's critically important to understand.

Think about it – if you're paying a 20% interest rate and carrying a balance of $10,000, how quickly does that interest expense add up? Using simple math, the interest accrues at $167 each month. If you are making a $200 payment . . . you will be trying to pay off that balance FOR-EVER! You don't want that.

You want to be able to pay it off every month

Another big benefit to having a business credit card – take advantage of the rewards. For example, I have a remodeling business I work with that spends roughly $400,000 a year on materials. With 2% cash back, that is $8,000 a year of free money!

As I alluded to earlier, make sure you read the fine print because some cards will give you 2% rewards (or sometimes even more) but there's a cap on the amount you can earn.

So, for example, if you're going to spend $400,000 like my remodeler client, but they are only going to give you cash back on the first $50,000 spent, that obviously makes a huge difference – only $1,000 (2% of $50k) vs. $8,000 (2% of $400k) without a cap!

Side note – you can use that free money as your vacation fund. That is precisely what my remodeling client does. He and his wife use that money every year to go on vacation. As he said –

"Hawaii, here we come!" ✤

The other powerful thing a business credit card can do is a little more complex to explain – it improves the timing. Let's say you have a manufacturing business and you are buying inventory to make your widgets. You buy the inventory on day 1 and you get an invoice that is due in 30 days. You wait until day 29 and pay for it but you don't pay for it with the check . . . you pay with your business credit card.

You've had that inventory to make widgets for 29 days. Depending on the billing cycle of your credit card, you likely have an additional 30-45 days before you have to pay cash to settle that credit card balance. At the end of the day, you bought inventory on day 1 but you're not actually laying out the cash for that inventory until 60-75 days later! Now, THAT is powerful and has a massive positive impact on your cash flow.

Depending on how long it takes you to make your widgets and sell them, quite possibly you have sold your widget and received cash from the sale before you even lay out money for your materials! You've actually swung your cash flow back the other way where you're getting paid for things before you even have to pay for them. Obviously, you have labor and admin costs as well, but as far as just the raw materials piece of that, you have created a huge advantage. So definitely, definitely, definitely look into utilizing a business credit card.

Another tip I want to mention is to accept credit cards. I know some businesses don't want to pay the 2-3% processing fee. However, when you look into the overall cost, you'll likely quickly see it makes sense to accept credit cards. First of all, it eliminates the collection process. You don't have to worry about getting a check. You're not wasting your time being a "check chaser".

In addition, according to a recent study, people spend 12-18% more money when they use a credit card as opposed to using cash for their purchase[13]. You'll spend 12-18% more if you're using a credit card because it doesn't seem as real. If you have to pull cash out of your pocket or write a check and hand it to someone, that is real.

Consider this – if you are going out to dinner and you take $50 in cash with you to pay for dinner, you know you have a finite amount of money to spend – in this case, $50. Therefore, you will be mindful when ordering your food and drinks. Otherwise, you know when the check comes it will be a very embarrassing situation. However, if you are paying with a credit card, there are no immediate ramifications if you spend $60 instead of your budgeted $50.

If you're accepting credit cards, you're going to benefit from that consumer effect. Not only will they potentially spend more, but

---

[13] https://www.nerdwallet.com/blog/credit-cards/credit-cards-make-you-spend-more/

they will also be much quicker to whip out a credit card to settle their obligations vs. handing over cash or writing a check.

By the way, your customers may be trying to do the same thing I mentioned earlier that you should do (maybe they read this book before you – haha) – they may want to pay their business bills with a business credit card so they can take advantage of delaying the cash outlay as well as accumulate additional cash back rewards.

I'll give you a quick example on this to illustrate from a numbers perspective why it makes sense . . .

Let's say you have a $1,000 invoice so the credit card processing fees associated with that payment would be $30 (presuming 3%). Now, think about what a negative cash flow impact it has on your business when someone pays you late.

What about collections? You have someone in your business that part of their function (or maybe even their entire responsibility) is doing nothing but collections – calling people trying to get payments, chasing checks, etc. How much is their time worth? And if it's you,

How much is <u>your</u> time worth?

If you're a small business owner, you're already wearing a lot of hats. You might be wearing the collection hat, unfortunately. If it's taking you away from making additional sales (and maybe you are the only salesperson in your company), think about the impact that has. It's huge. In this example, it will only cost you ~30 bucks to eliminate all of those negative impacts. For almost all businesses, it's a no-brainer that you should accept credit cards. Frankly, you can (and should) bake that 2-3% into your pricing.

The next operational change you can make to get to the top of the "pay pile" is to establish a written credit policy. Right up front when you get a new customer, if you give them a copy of your written credit policy, that shows them you're serious. It also shows them you're going to monitor it. As they say, the squeaky wheel gets the oil.

Think about your business – if you have ever experienced a cash flow situation where you have a bit of a challenge . . . you get to the end of the month and you realize you only have $5,000 but $8,000 in the bills. (Hopefully, you are closely monitoring your numbers throughout the month so you know your situation well before monthend.)

Who are you going to pay? You can't pay everyone. Well, guess what? If you have a written credit policy and you've shown them you're serious about that, they know they better put your company at the top of the "pay pile". Otherwise, they know they're going to hear from you.

Let's talk about a couple things I recommend you have in your written policy. You can include a whole slew of things but, at a minimum, I recommend these items.

First of all, spell out that if you have to incur attorney fees to go to court to collect payment, who's going to pay for that expense. Of course, you should put that onus on the delinquent customer. This demonstrates how serious you are about it.

Payment terms, of course, go right up front.

- When is the balance due?
- Do you offer discounts?
- Are there late payment penalties?

Along those lines, you should outline those items transparently. I also suggest an incentive to pay early. Make it small – maybe a 1-2% discount for early payment, however, make the "early" part be worth your while.

One thing I will say regarding late fees – a big one here – in most cases, don't make it a flat fee. I've seen other businesses where they say, for example, if you're late, it's 20 bucks. If I have a bill with you and it's $50 and you're going to charge me a $20 late fee, that's 40%! I'm not going to be happy about that. And, frankly, it's not fair.

By the same token, if you have a bill that's $10,000 and you're only going to charge me $20 for being late and I'm prioritizing who I can pay that month, I'm going to pay you late because it's not that big of a penalty. Therefore, make it a percentage. A fair amount would be 2% per month (check local and state limits). If you want to be more aggressive, you can do so by making the penalty progressive. You might say it's 2% for late days 1-10, days 11-20 add another 1%, etc. It depends how aggressive you want to be. Of course, always check your local regulations to determine limitations where you do business.

What I would say though is, much like parenting, don't make rules that you don't intend to follow. If that is your policy, don't let them off the hook or they're going to see you're not serious and then later they're going to not pay you and expect the same treatment. In addition, you could open yourself up to possible legal action for not applying your credit terms uniformly. Always do the right thing!

To combat persistent late payers (aside from requiring up-front payment or firing them as a customer), you could write a different type of progressive penalty into your policy. You could start out at 2% per month but if they are late two consecutive months, your new late payment penalty becomes 3% and so on.

The last thing I want to mention in regards to operational changes you can implement to improve your cash flow is to only pay your bills when they're due, no sooner. The only exception to that is if there is a discount offered for early payment. If they offer you a 1-2% discount for paying earlier, definitely take advantage of that if your cash position allows it. Even still, if the discount is within 15 days, pay on day 14. Don't pay earlier. Wait as long as you possibly can, without being late, to pay the invoice.

Aside from a discount, if it's due in 30 days, pay on day 29. Heck, you could pay on day 30 for that matter. I usually pay 1 day ahead of the due date. It's important because it helps stretch out your payables. As I mentioned earlier, if you wait until day 29 and pay with your business credit card, you can also take advantage of the further delay in paying off your credit card on top of that. It's a big, big advantage for you.

Further, if you use online bill pay, you can log-in early in the month and schedule to pay the bill on a later date, say the 29th. This allows you to mostly automate the process. You don't have to remember to log-in on a specific day to pay the bill, nor do you have to try to estimate mailing time if you're sending a check.

"That sounds great, Mr. Biz. However, my bank does not offer online bill pay."

When you have problems, Mr. Biz has your solutions!

If that is the case, you can utilize a 3rd-party service, such as bill.com.

Those are some operational changes you can make to improve your cash flow. Most of them are things you can implement in a short period of time that will drastically improve your cash flow situation.

Chapter 4

MINIMIZE COLLECTIONS TO MAXIMIZE CASH FLOW!

The first thing I'll mention is to automate your collection process as much as possible. Collections are a pain in the butt. Everyone knows that so the more you can automate them, the better. You want to make the process as seamless as possible. For example, setting up automated e-mail reminders to be sent on designated days – things like that.

Again, I don't get paid by QuickBooks (but I might be open to being an endorser, QB ®) but a lot of small businesses use that software so I will mention it. You can integrate QB with their preferred payments vendor to make efficiency improvements. The scheduled reminders show your customers you're serious about your Accounts Receivable and that gets your invoice moved to the top of the "pay pile".

For example, if your customer gets an e-mail reminder twice before your invoice is due – maybe seven days ahead and again at two days ahead – then, if necessary, you also make a phone call the day before the due date, I promise your efforts will pay huge dividends! If you have to make the phone call, you can use it as an opportunity to ask if they want to pay right then and there. They will likely appreciate the convenience: win-win! If you get voicemail, make your voicemail concise with simple instructions on how to pay the bill.

The effort demonstrates you're paying attention and that's how you ensure you're at the top of the "pay pile" and not on the "not gonna happen this month" pile. I promise – when a customer has a cash flow issue and they're trying to determine what bills they will pay (because they can't pay them all), these steps will get you on that "pay pile".

Obviously, that's the goal and what we want

The next tip I want to highlight, and this seems kind of obvious, but there are a couple of nuances to it . . . clearly assign collections responsibility to someone in your company. That obviousness aside, a common mistake I see made in many companies I have worked with is they assign this to a receptionist . . . because no one else wants to do it and, unfortunately, the receptionist draws the short straw.

The problem is, it doesn't get done because the receptionist is answering the phones, booking appointments, greeting customers and handling a myriad of other functions. As you know, the receptionist often becomes the catch-all for "other duties" – i.e. We need someone to do XYZ . . . hmmm . . . how about Bob (the receptionist)??

As I mentioned previously, most people don't like to do collection work. What do people do with things they don't like to do? Of course, they procrastinate those tasks and they don't get done or, at best, they get done with sub-optimal effort. This task is too critical to be completed with less than a concerted and focused effort.

Another issue with collections – make sure the collection owner is given clear objectives and, even more importantly, you provide them the bandwidth to be able to accomplish those stated objectives. You might even think about offering a small incentive based on their collections performance. This gives them goals to achieve with a vested interest in achieving them. In short, it gets them thinking and acting like an owner, which is what we want.

With an incentive, they are rewarded for doing the "tough" work and they can possibly make a little extra money based on their performance. At the same time, it's something that will still be overtly profitable for you as a business owner.

Yet another possible option is to make the collection owner be the sales person for that particular account. Further, you could tie that into the salesperson's compensation. If they sell to a customer and the customer doesn't pay, they don't get paid a commission on that sale until the customer pays. This gives your salesperson a vested interest in ensuring their customer pays in a timely fashion. Can you say, "thinking like an owner"? ©

And, by the way, they have an established relationship with that customer so it's a much easier collection conversation.

I'll give you one quick example –

I worked with a ~$5 million medical practice and their process was that they asked for payment up-front when services were rendered. This is typical in their industry. I'm sure we have all seen signs stating as much in a doctor's office.

Unfortunately, there were a fair amount of people that couldn't pay up-front. In those instances, the practice would send a letter at 30 days past due, at 60 days past due and at 90 days past due, then . . . [waiting] . . . [crickets] . . . they would do absolutely nothing. "Oh well – they didn't pay. Darn the luck!"

So, 2-3 months before they hired me, they wrote off over $300,000 of accounts receivable that had just been sitting there . . . growing and growing and growing . . . over an extended period of time. Those patient accounts had received the three letters over the initial 90 days but nothing further was done to collect the past due account. Once those past due accounts reached a critical mass, they were written off. In this case, to the tune of $300,000+!! UGH!

That brings us to the next piece of guidance – I recommend utilizing a collection company at 91 days past due. You want to expend your own concerted efforts (and be fair to your clients) during the initial 90 days. However, statistics show that at that point, your potential for collection success (without expertise) plummets dramatically. Unless your company is large enough – don't consider until you have at least ~$6 million in annual revenue – you don't want to pay to have your own collection group.

More than likely, being a collection expert is (WAY) outside of your company's core competency. Therefore, until you grow big enough you want to leave this to the experts who do this as part of their core competency.

If you do partner with a collection agency, always pay a percentage of collected dollars and not a flat rate. It is tempting to pay the low flat fees. However, think about it – at that point the collection agency already has their money. Potentially, they could care less if they collect any of your money! You would hope they would do the right thing but can you guarantee how much effort they will put forth for an account on which they have already been paid?

They have no incentive to collect that money for you

On the flip side, if they don't get paid until they collect money for you . . . do you know where that leads us . . . [wait for it] . . . they think like owners!

That being said, do your research to make sure you find a good company! As you may have heard, there are many unscrupulous companies that do a lot of shady things and treat people inappropriately. Even though they owe you money, you don't want your customers to be subjected to that treatment. You just want them to pay you.

The last piece on that – if you hire a collection company, don't pay more than 40%. I know of reputable collection agencies that absolutely do things the right way while delivering top-notch performance and they charge 40% at the minimum volume. Depending on the volume you send their way, you can negotiate downward but, again, you should never pay more than 40% for that expertise.

Next, and this sounds obvious but I don't see it happen often enough – sort your accounts receivable by amount, in descending order, not by days past due or alphabetically. Start with the big hitters! You get the most bang for your buck that way. Your largest past due balances get the most attention. That's important to remember.

This is an easy one – I alluded to this previously but make sure you're reaching out to your clients before the invoice is due. Some people suggest calling early on, but I think that's a bit on the aggressive side for my taste, especially with established customers.

It's happened to me before where an invoice is due in 30 days. Anyone who has heard me talk before knows I recommend, unless a discount is offered, you pay it on day 29 (presuming net 30 terms). If you call five days ahead of time, they may tell you – "I've got four days left to pay this. I'm not late. Stop bugging me."

I would recommend e-mailing them five business days before the due date. At that point, don't forget to remind them if you have a late penalty. That puts additional urgency to the situation and likely gets them on the ball.

You can, if still unpaid, remind them again one business day prior to the due date. For this reminder, especially if it is a troublesome customer, I recommend a phone call. As I mentioned earlier, offer to take payment right then on the phone, which is wildly effective at that stage in the process.

Once they are past due, another reminder is necessary. With this reminder, be sure to alert them to the new amount due, presuming you have a late fee penalty. The last thing you want to do when you receive payment is haggle with them because they didn't include the late fee. If you take the path of least resistance and let it slide, they will remember that and they'll never take your collection efforts serious again.

Do not let that happen!

Payment terms are what they are and you need to apply them consistently. You could even face litigation for not applying your terms equally to all customers. Do not expose yourself to undue and unnecessary risk – adhere to your terms unequivocally.

If you find yourself often wanting to give customers a break on the terms, consider altering them to reflect your new mindset. However, payment terms are not something you want to constantly alter. Do your research and thoughtfully construct your terms, then stick to them.

Make sure your collection owner is properly prepared for collection calls. First of all, you want to be prepared to take payments – either ACH their account or charge their credit card. Those are, in order, the best resolutions. Make it easy for your customers to pay you. It sounds simple but it expedites payment like you wouldn't believe.

I also mean being ready for the excuses as to why they haven't paid you. It's akin to the experienced salesperson – they have an answer for every reason why you won't or can't buy.

- You tell them you don't have enough money – "Well, we can put you on a payment plan".

- You tell them you need to think it over so they create urgency – "If you buy today, I will give you a 10% discount".

For example, if a past due account says, "Oh, sorry I was late. The check's in the mail". You want to have a script ready to respond to that and say something like – "OK – great! Can you please tell me the check number?" Oftentimes, as the cliché' goes, the "check's in the mail" means the check's <u>not</u> really in the mail. If you determine that, it will allow you to ask some additional questions to find out what's really going on. They might say they're not happy with the product (or service) and that's why they haven't paid you.

Granted, they may not have even reached out to you at this point to communicate their dissatisfaction. It might not actually be that they're unhappy but they're using that as an excuse to not pay you. So, have a response on the ready to address that situation.

At least initially, you want to give them the benefit of the doubt and be in "dispute resolution" mode. Approach it with a high level of customer service to resolve any issues – whether real or otherwise.

I will tell you at least half the time that happens they're not really unhappy. They're just trying to make an excuse to not pay you or not pay on time. As you delve into it, it might be they're having a cash flow problem of their own.

As we all know, that is a common pitfall for all small business owners. But, since you are reading this book, you will be a Cash

Flow Pro and you might even be able to provide some guidance that leads them out of their cash flow doldrums. If you do that, three things will happen:

1) You will make a friend for life.
2) You will get paid sooner for that invoice.
3) Due to their gratitude for your insightful advice, they will likely always put you at the top of their "pay pile" from that day forward.

OK – back to the problem at hand . . . other than offering your cash flow expertise, you can do a couple of different things with that. You can ask them to send you a post-dated check (but only if they know with certainty it will clear), then you can hold it until the date of the check. It's all about resolving that past due account, baby! Post-dated checks aren't exactly my favorite tool to use but they are definitely better than their diabolical cousin, Mr. No-Check-For-You! (A respectful tip of the cap to Seinfeld's Soup Nazi)

Alternatively, you can assess how bad their financial situation is and, with your newfound cash flow prowess, determine the best course of action for both parties.

- Would a payment plan work?

- How can we do this to help each other out and resolve the situation?

- Is a partial payment the best solution?

- What is a reasonable partial payment amount for both parties? Partial payments stink for you but partial is better than receiving nothing and having to write-off the entire balance!

If you have to resort to one of these methods to resolve the situation, at a minimum, you need to alter your payment arrangement with that customer (if you continue doing business with them). Every customer relationship is unique and you have to go with your gut. However, unless you have a long-established relationship with the customer, you should strongly consider severing ties with them.

If you maintain the relationship, to protect your company you do need to implement more stringent payment terms. Optimally, these more aggressive terms are already spelled-out in your payment terms.

For example, you should have progressive terms that enable you to apply more aggressive measures to customers with whom you have had prior collection challenges. Depending on your tolerance, you could, for example, delineate 3 levels with the payment terms dependent upon each customer's payment status:

- Level 1: payment due in 30 days

- Level 2: (with a late payment >10 days): 50% payment due up-front; remaining 50% due in 20 days

- Level 3: (with >1 payment issue): 100% due up-front

You may be thinking – "Mr. Biz – that sounds great but I'm reasonably certain my customers will not go for those terms." That is the beauty of this – you are in control!

Set the terms to the appropriate level of nuisance you are willing to accept and nothing more. As a benchmark, set the terms at the level at which you would be OK with your client walking. I don't mean that in a dismissive way at all. You need to determine two things here:

1) Your level of tolerance for non-payment.

2) Your profitability.

For example, if you are the "check chaser", you need to calculate what your time is worth. If a past due account calls and says they have a check for you, but you have to drive 60 minutes round-trip, what is your time worth?

[Side note – this is yet another reason why ACH'ing accounts and/or accepting credit cards are important options at your disposal.]

To give you some quick math on that – if you pay yourself $30 an hour and we throw in 20% for benefits, you just spent $36 to pick-up that check. More importantly, you "wasted" an unproductive hour driving to pick-up a check while you could have been doing something else! [And you're worried about paying 2-3% in credit card fees??]

Are you the only salesperson in your company?

Let's say, for the sake of argument, you go through this exercise twice per week. In a year, you just "spent" almost $4,000 of your company's dollars **AND** you also "spent" 104 hours of time. If you are the only salesperson, how many sales could you make happen in 104 hours?

Let's say it takes 4 hours per sale . . . that's 26 sales. And, let's say each sale equals $5,000 annually.

You are wasting $134k every year on chasing checks!

Can you believe that?! The numbers quickly become staggering. Would you like an additional $134k in revenue?

This is my favorite – "I never got an invoice". Well, I guess that could be the case in some situations but I think most companies are on the ball enough because they want their money and they want to make sure their cash flow is in good shape. Obviously, you want to confirm – we emailed it to you on 'x' date to the attention of so-and-so. I would speculate greater than 70% of the time they did receive the invoice. It's another stall tactic.

Lastly, what I'll say in being prepared for the collection calls is to have an escalation process. At what point does your collection person escalate it and what sort of leverage or leniency do they have on their end to be able to say – "OK, can you pay me 90 percent?" At what point do you give in a little bit and what sort of leeway does your collection person have to negotiate settlements

Fact is, there are a ton of small business owners that use QuickBooks. As many of you know, there is a "Pay Now" button you can use in that software package. "Pay Now" will automate your billing and your collections. It reduces the amount of time it takes to get paid. Period.

If you have QuickBooks already (and I'm not suggesting run out and get QuickBooks if you don't have it), but if you have QuickBooks and you're struggling with this, I recommend looking into it. I, personally, deal with several small businesses myself and I actually prefer it.

I prefer when they send me an e-mail with the "Pay Now" button (regardless of the vendor). Literally, when the e-mail comes, there's a button – you click on it, then the checkout screen pops up. You input your credit card information, you click a button and you're done. It's a <u>seamless</u> process.

As I regularly recommend, the more you can make it easy to do business with your company, the faster you will get paid. It helps out businesses on both ends. It helps dramatically decrease your accounts receivable aging. You're shortening up the process and collecting the money.

Incent your customers or clients to pay early and make sure you have a penalty for paying late. For example, if you typically give 30 days to pay, maybe you offer if they pay within 5 or 10 days (shorten it enough to make it worth your while), they receive a 1-2% discount. I always advise my clients if there's a discount to be had, take it unless you're in an absolute dire cash flow situation. Any discount you can get, you should absolutely take advantage of it.

Again, make sure you spell this out on your invoice. On the flip side of incenting to pay early, you make clear the penalty for paying late. Almost always make the penalty a percentage of the cost of the invoice and not a flat fee. Literally, on the invoice clearly spell those out. When the initial invoice goes out – if you pay by this date, you get a 1-2% discount. Or if you pay after whatever the date is you pay 'xyz'.

Typically, I recommend a 2% per month penalty. On an annual basis, that's ~24%, which is slightly more than what you're going to pay for a business credit card. However, considering the situation, it's a fair rate. Hopefully, you don't get into the situation where you have to use it.

If you have a troublesome customer with whom you need to be more aggressive, you can even make the penalty progressive. For example, the penalty is 1% for each 10 days they are late. So, if they are 30 days late, the penalty is 3%.

Always check your local regulations to ensure you are in compliance

I cannot emphasize enough – accept credit cards! I know people are often hesitant, especially in a very small business, to pay that 2-3% fee. I will tell you the research has shown it is absolutely worth it. With a credit card, it makes it so much easier to do business with you. You may find a company that has a cash flow problem so they can't necessarily write you a check but they're willing to put it on a credit card. Down the line, if they're not going to pay that credit card, that's their issue, not yours. They may be trying to use a business credit card to stretch out that payables cycle (per Mr. Biz).

They may want to use that credit card to pay so they can get another 4-6 weeks before they have to actually lay out cash to pay for that material or service. That's another way accepting credit cards is a win-win for you and your customer!

I hope these tips will help you minimize your collections while maximizing your cash flow!

Chapter 5

WHAT TO EXPECT WHEN YOU NEED FINANCING

In this chapter, we're going to address a topic I frequently hear from business owners – Financing! First, let's walk through an overview of the various options.

For short-term loans, you can start with the Small Business Association (SBA). The SBA gives loans and they're typically going to be a little more lenient with some of the business terms. For long-term loans, of course, you can connect with a bank or credit union. Be mindful of the fact that when dealing with SBA/bank/credit union, the application process is usually going to be a little more complex.

Credit cards might be a viable option if your needs are very short-term – i.e. you can pay off the balance when it becomes due in 4-6 weeks (depending on your billing cycle timing). It's important to ensure you do not allow your credit card debt to continue building. It can quickly spiral out of control on you.

Before you know it, the payment you can afford to make each month doesn't even cover the interest that is accumulating. So, even if you are no longer increasing the balance with additional charges, the balance is still building – ouch! That might sound a little confusing so let me illustrate it:

Credit card balance	$25,000
Monthly interest	375
Monthly payment	300

As you can see here, your balance would grow by $75 each month without any additional charges. In addition, you will be paying interest on that incremental $75. As this compounds, the gap widens and the balance grows by more than $75 each month. Further, at some point you could run up against your credit limit.

Another possible short-term option is invoice financing. This could prove to be a great periodic resource for businesses that bill at milestones for projects and, therefore, go extended periods of time between customer payments. As with other short-term options, if it turns out you need to utilize this option on a regular basis, you might want to consider other options. First, I should mention another commonly used term for it is "factoring".

How does factoring work?

I'll explain briefly: let's say you have sent an invoice for $10,000 to your customer but they haven't paid you yet and maybe you know they are notoriously slow payers. In the meantime, you need cash to pay your business expenses – perhaps salaries for your employees working on the project? A factoring company will loan you money against that invoice. They will receive payment directly from your customer, take their cut, then disburse the net proceeds to you.

As with any financing vehicle, the terms vary but they will typically give you up to 80% of the invoice amount, then charge you for loaning you that money. As an example, they might charge you 1% of the loaned amount for every ten days until the invoice is paid by your customer. With that in mind, if you anticipate your customer might take six weeks to pay the invoice, this is probably *not* a good option. In that case, you'd want to use something like a business line-of-credit (LOC) or something along those lines. It's something that should only be used short-term and sporadically. However, it is absolutely a solid option in certain circumstances.

Let's say you expect to receive payment from your customer in the next five days, but you are short on cash and you have a payroll run in two days. In most cases, they can issue a disbursement quickly, especially if you bank with one of their partner banks. In that instance, you can wait to receive the money as late as possible to delay starting the interest accumulation.

I'm sure some of you can appreciate how this could be helpful for you. Consider an IT company working on a 6-month project with an overall cost of $100k. In that instance, I would recommend more frequent milestones. However, let's presume they have 3 milestones over the 6-month project duration. If they invoice on day 60 but don't get paid until day 105 (30-day terms

+ 15 days late), they have incurred ~3.5 months of expenses for the project without being paid a dime. This presumes they didn't receive anything upfront, which, in most cases, I recommend.

Nonetheless, to put this example into perspective, suppose that IT company had an $80k per year resource working full-time on the project. Even only including salary & benefits for that resource (and no OT), through 3.5 months they would have spent $28,000 with no customer payments to offset against it! If you don't have adequate reserves to cushion that blow, it will kill your cash flow.

Again, though, if that is how the project lays out, including the expected late payment, I would recommend more frequent milestones. In addition, be sure to clarify with the client the precise accounts payable process on their end. That way you can hopefully expedite receiving payment from them with the process you use to invoice them. To whom to send the invoice? Will an emailed invoice suffice? Are they comfortable paying via credit card or ACH'ing their account?

While those details may seem trivial on the surface, they can be pivotal in decreasing the accounts payable process. As I often say – make it easy for your customers to do business with you. Everyone likes easy.

Sorry, I got off on a bit of a cash flow tangent. Sometimes I can't help myself. OK – I digress . . .

What I want to do now is focus on whether or not you're going to deal with a bank and what does a bank look for when you want to borrow money from them. The initial piece you're going to need to do is determine the loan amount you want. Typically, if you're looking for a smaller loan amount, banks usually aren't the best option. No, it isn't because banks don't like small businesses. Banks spend basically the same amount of time servicing a $5 million loan as they do for a $10,000 loan. Clearly, they make a lot more profit on the $5 million loan. They are running a for-profit business and are accountable to their shareholders after all.

Often people say,

"Banks are terrible; I can never get a loan!"

and/or

"The rates are terrible!"

It's not that banks are terrible, although the rates might be. I should say, it's more so that they price themselves accordingly. For a small loan amount, they price it to ensure they're still going to earn at least a minimal profit.

Without getting too far into the weeds, it also depends how their overall loan portfolio is structured. In simple terms, smaller loans might be preferable at times and, therefore, their rates would be more attractive. Other times, not so much, and that's when you see non-competitive rates. When that occurs, what they are in effect saying is, we don't want those loan types . . . unless you are willing to pay handsomely for the money.

Another piece to consider is the purpose of the loan. The more specific you can be, the better. If you need the money to purchase equipment, your lender will want to know what type of equipment you're buying; how you're going to use it; what the life expectancy of that equipment is (they will determine this); and what type of revenue that equipment's going to generate for you. Preparation is key here. Otherwise, at best, you delay the loan approval process; at worst, you could damage your chances of getting approved. These days, the loan process is mostly a complex mathematical equation, including items such as:

- What is your credit rating?

- Does your current operating financial performance meet their criteria?

- How much debt do you already have?

- How long have you been in business?

- Is your industry foreseeably at risk to external factors during the loan term?

- Etc.

These and other factors are scored, weighted and risk-adjusted (to account for best- & worst-case scenarios) to determine not only your creditworthiness, but also the amount they are willing to loan you and the rate you receive. However, with a small lender, being prepared & on the ball just might push you into a higher rated category and help you get the loan, get a higher loan amount or maybe even a lower interest rate. Bottom line, it never hurts to be prepared.

If you want the money to hire additional resources, they're going want to know how many people, & what they will do. Part of the reason they want to know these things is to make sure the loan amount you're requesting matches up for the *purpose* for the loan. If you're going to hire three people to be a cleaning crew and you are requesting a $400k loan . . . that is going to raise a red flag.

Some of that is to make sure you're not doing anything shady. It's also to help them help you to determine what loan option is best. There are several different options, but which one makes the most sense based on the purpose and amount? Those are a few of the things that banks are going to want to know from you right away.

All right... let's dive further into things the banks look at when you apply for a loan. They're going to want to know the type of entity you have. Generally speaking, small businesses can be organized in four different ways:

- Sole proprietorship
- Partnership
- Limited liability company (LLC)
- Corporation

There are a few different types of corporations as well. From a lender's perspective, knowing how your company is organized can provide insight into how you operate your business. In some cases, lenders will add a "surcharge" for sole proprietorships and partnerships because they prefer working with an LLC or a corporation. This is primarily because these businesses have more legal protections and are less likely to fold if the owner faces a lawsuit or financial setbacks. For example, if you're a sole proprietorship and you lose a personal lawsuit that wipes you out financially, that will likely necessitate shutting down your business.

Something else a lender will want to know is do you have a business plan. The correct answer, of course, is – Yes!". As you could guess, their next request will be to see it. As with a few previously mentioned items, depending on your lending source, not having a business plan could delay your loan approval process. If you skipped this step when you started your business, I would recommend creating one, even if just a simple version. In fact, once you create it, re-visit it periodically as your business evolves.

Some people suggest a business plan should be 30-50, or even 100 pages?! When I was working on my Master's degree, one of the key projects I had to complete was putting together a full business plan. That beast ended up being 124 pages! While it was "less-than-fun" at the time, it helped me recognize the importance of a business plan and how it can benefit the owner(s). Nonetheless, it can be overwhelming to consider.

However, like many things, you can Google it to find a template. Once you have the template, you can fill in the blanks to create it. Or, you can hire an expert to guide you through the process. Or, maybe just hire a business plan expert to review it when you're done. They can give you some critique and provide ways to improve it. A well-done business plan will definitely strengthen your loan application. Because so few small businesses have a well-done business plan – i.e. the bar is low – just having one will move you through the process more easily. Plus, as I alluded to earlier, I do recommend having one, even if you don't need it for a loan. You will be surprised how pertinent it is after you have it.

Among other things, they'll want to review:

- Sales projections – are they realistic?

- Expense projections – are they realistic?

- Are you profitable?

- If so, how profitable are you?

- How well can you cover current debt obligations?

- How will that change with a new loan?

- How accretive will the loan be to the business?

Everything that supports quantitative business goals are what they're going to want to see. They want to see the possible risks and opportunities you have identified (anything missing?), then how you plan to handle them if they occur. This is particularly important for a business that is 1-3 years old. If you've been in business for 10 years, a business plan becomes less important to a lender because you already have a 10-year track record in your rear-view mirror. You have faced several challenges, including riding through a full economic cycle. That proves more than just something on a piece of paper.

Here is an important element that is sometimes missed:

With the additional volume the loan proceeds will provide, have you considered the space needs you're going to have as you continue to grow? If you make widgets and you project the loan proceeds will increase production by 50%, does your current space accommodate that new production level. It's OK if it doesn't. You just need to account for it in your projections. For example, will you need to add-on to your current facility (if that's even possible)? Will you need to find a new facility? If so, have you researched those costs and included them in your projections?

But wait – there's more!

- If you do need a new facility, have you included the impact of moving costs and possible downtime while you move?

- If you have to break your current lease, have you quantified and included that cost?

- If you own your current space, but cannot expand as needed, how will you use that space?

- Will you lease it to another tenant? If so, how long will it take to attract a new tenant?

- Sell it? Same – how long will that take? What will be the proceeds?

- What if you have to carry it for a while after you relocate – i.e. you are paying for your current facility mortgage **and** the cost of your new facility at the same time?

These are just a handful of considerations to take into account. Net message – don't forget your space needs when projecting your numbers.

Sometimes, through no fault of your own, your industry can impact your credit worthiness. Think about it:

Every industry has different levels of risk

There are certain industries that lenders tend shy away from but that wouldn't impact most of you. Examples would be firearms or any type of adult entertainment business. The main reason, among others, for their hesitancy is those two examples could impact the lender's reputation. An investor or customer could see they lend to those businesses and say – "Oh geez, I can't do business with companies that are involved with those types of entities." No judgement here – just relaying a reason that could preclude that type of business from gaining a loan approval.

The lender will *always* take a conservative, risk-averse approach. Their underwriter's job is to protect their balance sheet from the worst-case scenario, whatever it is. Of course, they will risk-weight that worst-case scenario for the duration of the loan term to account for probabilities, etc. But, at the end of the day, risk management is the name of the game!

Another piece of info you're going to need, and hopefully are familiar with, is an employee identification number (EIN). Basically, that's a social security number for your business. Not all businesses need one, but you're required to have one if you have a corporation of employees, you have a multimember LLC, or if your LLC is going to be taxed as a partnership or a corporation. If it doesn't fall into one of those categories, you can just use your social security number for tax returns.

That said, you will need an EIN just to open a business bank account. Did I mention acquiring an EIN is free and you can apply online? Oh, and by the way, it takes a grand total of about 2 minutes. Taking those factors into consideration, why not just make it happen?

I promise it will make your life easier

I can speak from my own personal experience. It makes it much easier to have a separation between your personal and business finances. It is super-easy to apply online; it's free; and it takes ~2 minutes. As the folks at Nike say, "Just Do It".

Next up, they will want to know *any* and *all* types of business licenses and/or permits you have, if any. Using myself as an example, my businesses don't have any required type of licensing or permitting. However, there are many industries that do require them, such as, but not limited to: plumbers, electricians, HVAC, attorneys, financial planners, etc.

You might be wondering – why they heck would my lender care about *that*?! For the most part, there are two reasons:

1) Ensuring you are following the law, and
2) Ensuring you aren't putting your business at risk (if you do not have those pieces in place).

Without fail a lender is going to ask how long you have been in business and they will most definitely confirm your answer so don't embellish. The longer you've been in business, the better. It demonstrates your company's ability to weather the storm and overcome challenges. If it's <2 years old, it's not impossible to get a loan but it certainly limits your options. Mostly, banks are going to want to loan to a business that is over 2 years old.

I mentioned at the outset of the chapter that there are some alternative lending sources. Some of them only require 1 year (or less) of history to be comfortable loaning money. Outside of SBA loans, these options will likely be more expensive because the lender is taking on more risk. This is another instance where having that solid business plan behind you is critically important.

Another common question – does your personal credit score impact your company's ability to gain loan approval? Contrary to popular belief, it definitely does! They will also consider your business credit score but don't think for a second that your personal score doesn't factor into your creditworthiness.

First, let's talk about your personal credit score. They're going to ask for that for a few different reasons. They put a varying amount of weight if you handle your personal finances effectively. If so, the presumption is you're probably going to handle your business finances in the same manner. Of course, the amount of weight that carries in their loan decision depends largely upon your corporate structure, the options of which we discussed earlier in this chapter. How much personal liability do you have towards the business's debt?

A few general guidelines to be mindful of: you need to have a credit score of at least at 600; obviously, above 700 is better; if you have above that level, you're going to be fine. If you have a score lower than 600, you're probably going to have difficulty getting financing. If you do obtain financing at that level, the interest rate is going to be exorbitantly high. That isn't the lender being a jerk to you. They are actually just protecting themselves against the risk of you not re-paying your loan (based on your past creditworthiness).

<u>Bottom line:</u>
A good credit score creates less costly lending options

How does your business credit score play into this? Believe it or not, some people don't even realize their business has a credit score. Different events can trigger your business being listed for a credit score. Simple things such as opening a business bank account, which most, if not all, of you have done, will trigger it. Just like that, and maybe before you even realized it, your business has a credit file on record!

When you incorporate your business, that's going to trigger a credit file for your business. As mentioned earlier, obtaining an EIN will also establish a credit file for your business. Much like your personal credit, you don't need to do anything; it's automatically done.

There are three primary credit reporting agencies in the United States:

- Experian
- Trans Union
- Equifax

Like personal credit, your business's credit score measures how well you pay your bills –

- Do you pay timely?

- How much do you have outstanding?

- How much of eligible credit are you using?

- What type of credit do you have outstanding?

If you have business credit cards, they will be listed on your business credit report. For example, if you have two business credit cards and they each have a credit limit of $20k, they can see you have a *potential* to get $40k in debt with your business credit cards. Even if you have $0 balance on an open account, they will take that into consideration and assume that you *could* get yourself into deeper debt without them even knowing about it.

I'm sure you were expecting this at some point: yes, bank statements will likely be required. This will help the lender to verify deposits, which confirms revenue, etc. This also gives them insight into how well you manage the cash flow from your business. They want to know that you are managing it responsibly so you aren't getting yourself into a situation where you cannot pay your obligations in a timely manner. They want to feel confident you've got enough cash coming into your business and an adequate cushion to maintain your business operations during crunches.

Specifically, when the economy fluctuates and during your slow season, if you have a seasonal business, they want to make sure that you've got enough money to still make your loan payment. It's that simple. In a nutshell, they will test to see how your financials will hold up during a worst-case scenario. Your business may be humming along like a well-oiled machine right now but if your balance sheet is weak, it can quickly falter during an economic downturn. That's precisely what they want to measure: in a bad economic situation, how likely is it that you can continue paying back your loan with them.

At a minimum, you should expect they're going to ask for four months of your business bank statements. Honestly, they're probably going to require even more than that. In many cases, they will want two years of statements (or more). As I mentioned previously, if you don't have a separate bank account for your business yet, now's the time to get one! It's very helpful in keeping your personal finances separate from your business finances.

Of course, your prospective lender is also going to want to see your business financial statements – income statement and balance sheet, at the least. They will want up-to-date for the current year as well as prior years.

You should know – while it varies by lender, some will only lend you money if you are profitable. But then some might say, "Hey, we just have a minimum revenue requirement that ties to the amount you want to borrow". They will want consider a ratio in that case. For every $x thousand dollars of money borrowed, they will want to see $y thousand dollars of consistent and predictable revenue.

Another option that's the most lenient of the three options, especially if you are a startup, some lenders just look for an upward trajectory in your revenue. They're going to look to ensure you are continuing your upward trend. Frankly, what they're more than likely to do is compare that trajectory to your business plan and see how far off you were when you wrote your business plan. For example, you said, "We're going to grow

20% a month." Are you growing at 20%? Or, are you growing at 30%? Or – GULP – you're only growing at 2%!

If that's the case, they're going to look at your business plan with a little more of a critical eye because they'll see that it wasn't an accurate projection – either it was too aggressive or maybe your business isn't going as well as you'd anticipated. That will be concerning to them because it will cause them to not put as much weight into your overall projections in your business plan.

Next up is their review of your balance sheet – this gets a little into the accounting weeds, but simplistically, it is a snapshot of your business's financial health. It shows what you have in assets – items that have value could possibly be sold, if needed – and what are your liabilities – what you owe others.

Most people look at their balance sheet and think it's just a bunch of accounting mumbo-jumbo. However, it demonstrates an important view of your business and is *very* telling to a lender. As an example, they will review your accounts receivable (earned but not yet received revenue; this is an asset) and your accounts payable (unpaid invoices you owe others; this is a liability). Why the heck would they want to see that? These two items are going to show them how efficient your business is at receiving payment and paying your own bills.

These are directly related to your cash flow

If your customers are paying you late, but you have invoices due to your vendors, you can see where you can get into a pickle. If your accounts receivable aging shows you have too many past due accounts from your customers, it's going to appear that you're not being effective at collecting payment – which *could* be a bad sign, right? This shows your collection process isn't working as it should.

The accounts payable aging report is, as you can guess, the opposite. It's going to show the number of invoices that *you owe* others, as well as whether or not *you* have anything that's overdue. Make sure they're going to demonstrate that you pay your bills on time. Think about it – they are evaluating you to see if you will pay *them* back! If you aren't paying your current obligations timely, what will make them think you will treat them differently?

If you report your business as a pass-through entity on your personal tax return, they're going to want to see at least two years of personal tax returns. This will provide an additional level of comfort in regards to the legitimacy of your business financial statements.

You may also need to provide them proof of collateral and whether or not you already have a collateralized loan. Collateral is an asset you're willing to lose if you can't repay your lender. It "backs up" your loan and provides the lender another level of assurance in regards to what they can expect in a worst-case scenario. In other words, if you default on the loan, the lender can sell that collateral and then apply the proceeds toward your outstanding loan balance. Most alternative lenders don't require any type of specific collateral, but if you're applying for a bank loan or an SBA loan, they will want to know what kind of collateral your small business has to secure the loan. Collateral comes in many shapes and sizes – equipment, inventory, real estate, etc. Most assets that have value could be considered.

Of course, for equipment financing, the collateral is going to be the purchased equipment itself. A great example of loan collateral is when you take out a loan to purchase a car. The vehicle is collateral for the lender. If you stop making payments, they will repossess and sell it to help satisfy the outstanding balance.

If you have a commercial lease, they will want to see a copy of it. If you own your building, they will see that on the balance sheet in the form of an asset (the land and the building) and if you have a mortgage on the property, in the form of a liability (the loan). The reason they review your physical location situation is they want to make sure your business is going to be able to use that property for the duration of your loan term. They want to ensure your physical location will not cause a disruption in your business's success.

If you just have a "good ole boy" handshake agreement with your landlord, banks are not going to like that. It might sound great if, let's say, you are leasing from your friend, Bob. But what happens if something happens with/to Bob? If he has a bad situation in his personal life and has to liquidate the building, then the new buyer requires you to vacate. Or, what if Bob passes away, his heirs sell the property, and you are forced to move? What if you and Bob have a falling out and he evicts you? Clearly, each of those scenarios would have a detrimental impact on your business and possibly impede your ability to repay your loan with them That is exactly why the bank will want, and possibly require, you to have a formal lease agreement in place.

They likely will also want to review any type of binding legal contracts you have in place. These could be with major suppliers you have or other third parties. In fact, this would also include your operating agreement or your partnership if you have a franchise agreement. No, they aren't just being nosy by requesting this information. The theme is consistent with previously mentioned information – they want to ensure there is nothing in the contracts that could unknowingly have a negative impact on your ability to repay them. If they find something with which they are uncomfortable, they may even require you to alter language in an agreement in order to get approved for a loan.

They may also ask to review your payroll records for prior periods. They are primarily looking for two things here:

1) Are you completing your legally required payroll record-keeping duties?

2) Are you fudging payroll numbers in any statements?

The former shows you are not putting yourself at risk for a substantial government fine; the latter provides further assurance of your financial statement validity.

All right – just a few more things to cover on financing . . .

You will need to provide disclosure for any other debt you have. This would include open credit lines, like an unused business credit card. Again, you may be asking – why in the world would they want to know about a credit card with a zero balance? You have to remember they are considering your financial situation from a worst-case scenario. Just because that credit card has a zero balance now doesn't mean you won't run up a balance on it later – do you follow me? So, if that card has a credit limit of $25k, they might stress-test your financials considering the possibility you could have an incremental $25k in debt from this card.

The same goes for other credit instruments for which you have access. A line-of-credit (LOC) is a perfect example. Let's say right now you only owe $5k on your LOC but the limit on it is $100k. They will stress-test to take into account your access to that additional debt. Since it is already approved, you could borrow that additional money without them knowing. Obviously, increasing your debt by $95k, like in this example, would have a major impact on your financial situation.

You will also need to show details on any other existing debt. Things like:

- How much you owe
- Credit limit
- Interest rate

They will accumulate all of the debt information to calculate your debt service coverage ratio. That is a measure of the cash flow available to pay current debt obligations. The ratio states net operating income as a multiple of debt obligations due within one year, including interest, principal and lease payments. If you have a lot of debt already and your debt service coverage ratio is low, they may reject your application. Or, they may recommend you re-apply after you've paid down some of your debt. They want to make sure your incoming money is sufficient to pay the debt you currently have, as well as the additional debt you're possibly going to take on from them. As I alluded to earlier, they will also consider scenarios where you utilize *all* of your available credit – i.e. max out your credit limit on each debt instrument.

Last, but not least, they may ask about any type of ownership or affiliations you have. They'll want to know:

- If you have ownership in another business

- If you're a partner in other businesses

- If you're a board member

- If you're a consultant for another business

The reason for this is this will shine a light on *any* potential conflicts of interest the lender might have with issuing that loan as well as, on the flip side, your business may have with another company. That may be a positive thing if, for example, you have a sister company that feeds business into this business. This is why it is sometimes challenging when you try obtain a business loan and you have multiple owners. Just to let you know as a rule of thumb – the SBA usually checks personal financial information for *anyone* who owns at least 20% of the company.

In this last section, I'm going to hit you with some common mistakes I've seen people make when submitting a loan application.

The first thing you want to do is determine *why* you want a business loan. You need a *specific* reason. That's definitely going to affect the *types* of loans for which you're eligible. Different types of loans have higher risk associated with them, as you can well imagine. The second thing, is you want to calculate how much you can afford and it's not as simple as you may think. It needs to be calculated using at least some of the measures we have already talked about. For this step, a critical measurement is your debt service coverage ratio. You can roughly determine the size of the loan you can afford in the eyes of a lender.

Above all, it has to make financial sense for the lender. Let's say you really could afford a $30,000 loan and a monthly payment of a $1,000, but you're applying for $100,000. A bank is going to view that negatively. If you're willing to put yourself at risk by over-extending with a loan you cannot afford to pay back, you're not managing your finances responsibly. They're going to *know* you haven't done your homework and that could negatively impact your loan application.

Be sure to consider all of the different loan options available to you. The loan amount is going to help narrow those down, especially when taking into account your credit rating(s). Do some research before you even talk with a prospective lender. Alternatively, if you have a particular banker in mind, you might consider reaching out to them. Explain where you're at, what you're seeking, etc. and ask them to send you information on different options.

You want to make sure you are making a good choice for **you** and not just the choice the banker thinks you should choose. Hopefully, they have you best interest in mind, but some do not. They may push you towards a particular option because they are compensated higher for it. In addition, they might not fully understand the whole picture of what you're trying to accomplish and how your business works.

Only *you* are best at determining that

Next, gather all of the information we talked about. I advise you to consider more than one lender, but don't have any more than three. The primary reason for that is you don't want to have five different lenders perform "hard pulls" on your credit. That could actually lower your credit score! Make sure you've got all your ducks in a row. Each lender should have a checklist of requirements for you to follow. Have *everything* well documented and organized for them. This makes it easier for them to review your loan documentation. That creates a situation where they can process your application faster.

Finally, you've made it! Submit your application and celebrate with a few adult beverages! Just kidding (no, I'm not ☺). When you submit, it pays to review the checklist and your documentation with the lender. That way, if there are any issues, you can address them right then (or shortly thereafter). This could also expedite your process because you reduce the chance of delays due to your information. That said, as underwriters review applications, there are times when they might need additional information. An example of that might be an additional year of previous tax returns or financial statements.

What are some common mistakes *and* how do you avoid them? Some of these are *super* easy. But in the rush of everything, sometimes these get missed:

Don't submit any documentation that's blurry, unclear or incomplete. For example, when making a copy of a copy, the quality is sometimes less than acceptable. When an underwriter runs into something like that, they literally drop that piece of the review process and notify you of what they need. Net message – make it as easy as possible for them to review your application.

Be sure you're being transparent about the loan purpose. That will help them to help you the best. If you are using the loan to buy new machinery, outline how you expect the machinery will impact your business – quantify increased production or productivity, how much additional revenue do you project, etc.

Give them exactly what they need. For example, let's say they want three years of tax returns but you had a particularly bad year two years ago. Because of that, you decide to skip the bad year and give them another year back. They **will** notice and they **will** call you out on it. They do this for a living so they've seen it all. What impression do you think that leaves with them? At a minimum, that could cause them to review your documentation even more thoroughly, which will delay the process. Not providing enough or providing inaccurate information can definitely jeopardize your chance of being approved. There's never too much information in that situation.

Details are important! Double-check numbers – industry codes, addresses, phone numbers, bank account numbers, etc.

Don't miss deadlines

Just like when you're applying for a mortgage on the personal side, don't make any major purchases or make major changes to your business while your loan application is pending. Keep your financial situation stable and consistent.

OK – schwew! We made it through financing! Nice work!

It can be a tricky topic but one that most businesses experience at some point in their life cycle. My hope is when you reach that point this information will be helpful for you.

SECTION TWO

CREATING OPERATIONAL EXCELLENCE

Chapter 6

WHEN DIY GOES BAD

As small business owners, we are always on the lookout for ways to save money, right? I know I often utter words like this to myself – "I can do that. I'll do a little research and I'll be fine." Well, unfortunately, I can tell you from personal experience **and** from working with lots of small business owners, that is not always the best idea. Shoot – how many of you are guilty (like me) of even doing this with projects around your house? Mrs. Biz can attest to my penchant for, shall we say, biting off more than I can chew – DOH! The question we are going to address in this chapter is – when to hire an expert vs. when to do it yourself (DIY) to save money in your business?

As a small business owner, you wear many different hats. Everyone can relate to that. So, right off the bat, consider these questions:

- Do you *need* another hat to wear?

- Do you have time for that?

- Is the task something in which you have expertise/experience?

- What is your time worth vs. the cost of hiring it out?

- Will it take you away from revenue producing activities?

- What is the potential cost if you completely bomb in your efforts?

- What is the risk in that that scenario?

Saving money is great and everyone loves to do that. There are definitely some instances where you *think* you're going to save money, but in the end, because some of the potential issues mentioned above, it actually *costs* you more money. There are certain tasks that definitely should not be a DIY prospect. While there are a whole host of those, I want to hit on what I'll call, "The Big Four". I want to focus on these skills for two primary reasons:

1) They are most often skill gaps for owners.

2) They have the largest potential financial consequence, if done poorly.

You may be wondering what are "The Big Four"? OK – without further ado . . . drum-roll, please . . .

1) Strategic financial management
2) Legal
3) Marketing

4) Real estate

Boom – there they are! Don't DIY those tasks and you'll thank me for it later. See you in the next chapter . . .

Just kidding.

Let's dig into why I have anointed these four as I have. I will give you some food-for-thought as to the potential risks associated with trying to DIY them.

The biggest element I want you to recognize with these areas of expertise is you don't have to hire someone full-time for any of them. There are plenty of fractional resources available in each discipline. Meaning, you can hire them for as much or as little as you need them, nothing more-nothing less. Frankly, until your company reaches a certain level of complexity and/or revenue, you probably couldn't keep a full-time resource busy on a regular basis. You could for short bursts here and there – acquiring a new company (finance, legal), launching a new product (marketing), purchasing/leasing new space (real estate) – where you might need the resources close to full-time, but only on a short-term basis until those one-off tasks are completed.

I will admit a bit of bias here: let's first discuss strategic financial management. I don't intend for this to be a plug for my business, but explaining how I operate might sound that way. When you hire me (as an example) to help with your strategic financial management, you get a resource on your team that has 20+ years of experience in the CFO world, a Master's degree in Financial Management and experience helping lots of different types of businesses – all shapes and sizes – in many diverse industries.

You get a resource who has likely "been there-done that" on many challenges you face in your business.

And, as I mentioned, you only pay for what you need. My engagement level with each client is different and, consequently, so is what they pay me. It could be as simple as you only need me to help with cash flow, creating a budget, then preparing and reviewing a monthly financial package. I have had clients where I worked with them on some of those types of tasks, then over time it evolved into us just having a monthly strategic planning session. Of course, with the lower level of engagement, that is much less expensive for the business owner.

The point of me outlining those scenarios is to demonstrate two important considerations:

1) Hiring on a fractional basis gets you a well-experienced resource that likely has a great deal more expertise in their field than you do – i.e. huge value-add for your business, and

2) You only pay for what you need from them – i.e. not a heavy payroll burden. You can quickly and easily decrease this expense when you need to do so.

There are a few additional positives to consider with a fractional or part-time expert resource. The alternative would be to add someone on your staff. However, for what it costs to hire that expert fractional resource, you would have to hire someone with much less experience. With a fractional resource, they are just a 1099 so no benefits or employee issues with which to deal. If they are sick and cannot work, they don't get paid.

Finally, if you get to a point that you no longer need the resource, you can easily terminate the contract without the guilt you would have from terminating one of your employees. I don't mean that to be harsh towards the part-time resource but they likely have other revenue sources than just you so they should be fine. One of your employees solely relies on your company for their financial well-being.

But wait . . . there's more!

One additional positive to consider: unless you have expertise in any of "The Big Four", these resources should pay for themselves. Let me give you a quick example. Granted this is somewhat of an extreme situation, but it is a real-life example. With a recent client, during the first 90 days we created bottom-line improvements that gave them a 30x return on what they had paid me in those 90 days. That is a glowing example of what I mean when I say these resources should pay for themselves. Putting that into perspective: if I told you to give me $10,000 and within 90 days I'll give you $300,000 back, who wouldn't take that deal?! Of course, everyone would! Again, that is on the extreme side but it illustrates the power of choosing wisely on what **not** to DIY in your business.

My point is, you should expect they're going to more than pay for themselves. And then, at least on the financial side, you likely continue to reap those savings into perpetuity, right? You continue to see that money going forward.

Let's move on to the 2nd of "The Big Four" – *Legal*

Unless you are an attorney, I think this one goes without saying but you wouldn't try to represent yourself in court. You can't just *Google* that! However, there is more to it than just that.

There's a lot of that that goes into risk mitigation. Things such as: intellectual property protection – patents, copyrights, trademarks, etc. However, one legal risk that is prevalent for small businesses, but often overlooked – human resource (HR) issues/policies. It's critically important, especially in today's litigious society. Many people are "sue-happy", looking for a payday. Consider some of the seemingly frivolous lawsuits you have heard of that actually were awarded large sums of money?! All it takes is one person to feel wronged and they go to an attorney. Then, even if a lawsuit against you is not successful, how about the reputational risk associated with it? When people hear claims against you, even if they are later proven to be untrue, people initially presume you were doing something bad and that sticks with them. Maybe they never hear the final verdict? What is stuck with them is the initial false claims!

Let's say, for example, you own a medical practice and a patient claims they were sexually harassed. The patient speaks to an attorney who decides to gamble on a potential large payday by taking the case, even if it seems like a longshot. The attorney takes the allegations to the media and the accusations spread like wildfire. Even forgetting typical media – TV and radio – we all know how quickly out-of-the-ordinary stories can go viral on social media. Heck, maybe the accuser decides to protest outside of your practice's office? A year later, you are finally exonerated that nothing inappropriate occurred. However, in that 12 months' time, how many people have seen or heard about the initial claims and presumed guilt?

Let me ask you this – if you heard allegations like this against your child's pediatrician, would you wait for the court's decision and continue taking your child there? I'm guessing you would not. So, at the end of the day, what do these false allegations mean for your medical practice? It likely means you're out of business with a tarnished reputation. How do you quantify that financial impact? Would it be worth paying an attorney upfront?

Now, you might be saying – "That's a terrible situation but how could hiring an attorney help me?" An attorney, with their experience in the field (hearing about cases, knowing precedents, etc.), can advise you on appropriate procedures to have in place to help mitigate the risk of having this happen to your practice.

Too extreme and dramatic, you say? Take off your paranoia glasses, Mr. Biz! OK, how about this one . . .

You have a few disgruntled employees that claim they've been treated unfairly. You know how that scenario plays out – Gary Gossip starts complaining to another employee: "Can you believe 'xyz' happened? That's not fair at all!" Suddenly, their audience, who might not be otherwise triggered by their employer, gets pushed over the edge – "You're right, Gary! That is not fair! In fact, last month Betty the Boss said 'abc' to me when I know Sam did the same thing without being reprimanded!" Now, you have a potential firestorm brewing. Couple that with the fact that maybe employees aren't happy with the raises they got last month – "Owen Owner is making **TONS** of money and he can't even give us a 3% raise?!"

One of the employees has an attorney relative or friend to whom they confide how they, and others, have been wronged with inconsistent (or inconsistently applied) HR policies. The attorney finds out one of the "wrongly terminated" employees is in a protected class. Oh boy – this is quickly spiraling out of control.

Miss Attorney asks, "Hey, are there *other* employees there who are disgruntled?" Next thing you know, you've got 15 people in your company that are filing a class action lawsuit against you!!! All because you let one person slide a little on something! It sounds innocent enough but you just cannot do that. You have to actually have documented HR policies that adhere to the law, and equally important, you need to fairly apply them to everyone. As you read that, you probably thought – "No kidding, Mr. Biz. Tell me something I didn't already know." OK. Think about this –

- Do you have written HR policies?

- Has every employee signed off on having been given them?

- Have your HR policies been reviewed by an attorney well-versed in HR law?

- Have you cut a "favorite" employee some slack for something against policy?

Consider your answers to those questions and how any of them going sideways could impact your business. These are all things I have seen in reality. In fact, I would dare say they are much more common than you think.

As if that wasn't enough, I'll take it a step further to paint a more vivid picture . . .

What if a recently terminated employee accuses you of racism? Next thing you know, thanks to the attorney representing your former employee, the local news picks up on it. The station's consumer watchdog shows up with a camera outside of your place of business asking if it's true you condone racism?!?! The video of you denying it and telling them to get the camera out of your face is not a good look. Again, even presuming you are later exonerated, proving no racism ever occurred, the damage is already done. That reputational damage . . . how do you recover from that?

You won't believe this one . . .

I worked with a business that had almost this exact situation brewing in their office. When I alerted them to it at a Board meeting and told them we needed to right the ship, guess what I was told by one of the owners? I can't make this up . . . "We have insurance for that."

Wait – what? Are you kidding me?! To date, that is the only client I have ever terminated. I don't do business with people who operate like that!

Suffice to say, hiring expert legal help is critically important on many fronts.

The 3rd of "The Big Four" is *Marketing*

Perhaps more so than the 1st two of "The Big Four", you might be thinking you can handle this one on your own. You have a decent handle around it and you can trust Mr. Google to fill in the gaps, right? Unfortunately, probably not nearly as well as you think you can!

Before we even get into why it likely does not make sense to DIY your marketing, let me give you some guidelines to follow. I recommend spending 2-15% of your annual revenue. In reality, most small businesses I have worked with spend in 4-8% range. However, even in downtimes you should strive to spend at least 2% of your revenue. The 9-15% range would typically be a temporary situation. When should you consider that 9-15% marketing spend? Here are a few:

- Launching a new product/service
- Expanding your geographic reach
- Acquiring in-limbo customers from a failed competitor

That being said, you should expect a 300% return on whatever you do spend on marketing. If you're spending $10,000, you should expect to see a measurable bump in revenue of $30,000 overall.

OK – so why not DIY my marketing to save some coin?

Consider this quick example:

To keep the numbers simple, let's suppose you spend $10,000 a year on marketing and you decide to DIY it. You take your knowledge, do some Google research, talk to a buddy, wrap that all together and earn a 50% marketing return. Not too shabby, right? By DIY'ing it, despite your 50% return, you actually cost your company $5k, right? $5k in revenue - $10k in spend = -$5k. You're $5k upside down.

But what if you hired an expert . . .

What if you spent the same $10k on marketing, but hired an expert – someone who has ~20 years of experience and does this every day for a living – and they earn you my recommended 300% return? What does that look like? That same $10k spend earns you $30k in revenue. In that scenario, you are $20k on the positive! $30k revenue - $10 spend = +$20k. In this example:

DIY'ing is -$5k to your business.

Hiring an expert is +$20k to your business.

Comparing the two, for the same cost, the expert earns you an extra $25k!!

The bigger your marketing spend, the bigger the positive impact on your business. This is another example of when it does **not** make sense to DIY your business! Business owners need to be humbly self-aware of their level of expertise.

#4 in the "The Big Four" – Real Estate

Let's discuss real estate, then I've got a couple of what I'll call 'bonuses' that don't quite make "The Big Four", but they are important considerations.

For this one, I need you to do me a quick favor – take a quick peak at the expense section of your income statement. How much are you spending on real estate – rent/lease expense, mortgage expense, property taxes, property maintenance, property repairs, etc.? For most businesses, that is a top 3 expense. Typically, at the lowest it is 3rd, possibly behind people (salaries, benefits, et al) and raw materials. That makes it ripe for the picking (optimizing)!

If you've been paying attention this chapter, you know an example is coming your way. I have found examples are usually the best method for people to visualize different scenarios.

Typically, I have found total real estate expense for most small businesses is anywhere from 8-25%. Yes, that is a wide range but I'm just trying to give you an overall rule of thumb. Of course, this varies, depending on your business. A few influencing factors –

- Do your rent/lease or own?

- Are you a professional firm with higher average salaries, but perhaps higher rent costs?

- Are you a manufacturing company with more space, but also high raw material costs?

OK – so as not to disappoint with the expectations for an example, here you go . . .

Let's go middle-of-the-road and say your total expenses are $2 million and 15% of those are real estate in nature. That's $300k per year that are at stake. How much of a commercial real estate expert are you? How much experience do you have in negotiating a commercial lease? Do you know the per square foot rent amounts of other commercial spaces in the area? How about how much you should expect in lease improvements? If I lost you on *any* of that, please find an expert to help you! I'm serious. Let me show you why.

Again, I will base this example of what I have seen in real-life. If you tried to DIY it, you would probably be ecstatic with a 5%

savings, or $15k per year in this example. On the surface, that does sound great.

However, what if you hire an expert to help you, and they save you 20% (you may think that's a lot, but I'll explain that in a minute), that's $60k a year you would save by hiring an expert! Can you believe that? I'm not kidding! However, by not hiring the expert, you are potentially leaving a lot of money on the table. In this case, you are missing out on $45k every year! That's a lot of coinage, no matter how you slice it! You know the math, but I'll feel better outlining it – in barely over 2 years, that equates to $100k of savings! HEL-LO!!

But here's the BEST part!!

In most cases, you can hire a commercial real estate expert that won't cost even one penny out of pocket. How is that even possible? That can't be true?! Well, I'm here to tell you, it is true. The best way to explain it, for those that have purchased a home, it is somewhat akin to having a realtor as the buyer – the seller (landlord in this case) pays the fee of your realtor/real estate expert. You probably didn't know that, did you? For most, it is a "hidden gem" for small business owners.

Side note: if you don't know an expert in this space, please reach out to me. This is entirely too much money to leave on the table! I'm happy to connect you with someone in my vast network, if I can. No referral fees or any B.S. (I don't receive a dime from this) – just connecting you with, in most cases, a cost-free real estate expert.

These experts can often tell you info like I mentioned earlier:

- What are other tenants in your prospective building currently paying?

- What is the typical leasehold improvement budget included in your rate?

- Are either/both of these competitive with rates in the area for similar space?

If you're seeking a lease in a building, they can tell you things like: maybe they're looking to charge you $10/square foot, but other tenants in the building are only paying $8/square foot. In that case, the landlord is over-charging by 25%! Your real estate expert can save you money in that manner.

In the same way, they could also save you money when you're coming up for lease renewal. In a fair share of instances, especially if you've been a tenant for a while, they can negotiate improvements on your behalf. Without your expert, that improvement money would have come out of your own pocket!

OK – let's talk "bonuses" . . . what is important, but falls outside of "The Big Four"?

How about IT support? This doesn't impact as many small businesses because you may only have a couple laptops/printers, etc. However, I will say this from a personal experience perspective – there aren't many items as high on the frustration list for me as IT problems. Maybe I over-estimate my IT skills, which is likely. We rely so heavily on technology and when it doesn't function as we expect, WOWZA! Think about the last time your smartphone didn't immediately do what you expected it to do . . . super-frustrating, right? We are spoiled by the technological advances. We automatically expect our technology will work super-fast. If it doesn't . . . frustration quickly sets in, which is the primary reason I mention this area of expertise – IT.

Have you ever had difficulties printing a document? Printing seems simple enough, doesn't it? But, if it doesn't work when we click the 'Print' button, look out! I know it is very frustrating for me. Admittedly, maybe I am mentioning this particular area of expertise because it has been frustrating for me in the past. Funny thing is, and I've mentioned this before, I think I'm decent with IT issues. However, when an IT issue arises, I know my blood pressure rises. Subconsciously, I probably fear not being able to solve my IT problem so I dread it. If you suffer from that same IT-related anxiety, wouldn't it be nice to know you have a trusted IT resource you can call to help you? Watching YouTube videos only take you so far, right? ◉

OK – we are almost done here. I have one final area to mention that is a little outside of the box.

How about a virtual assistant?

Will you pay more per hour for a virtual assistant vs. the per hour of hiring a full-time resource? Yes, of course. However, you won't bear the full-time salary or benefits or sick time or retirement, etc. I have a contrary way of viewing the hiring of an administrative assistant resource . . .

I challenge you to look at it this way (bear with me here):

If you currently handle a fair number of administrative tasks **and** you're the primary salesperson for your company . . . how much time does hiring a virtual assistant (VA) free up for you?

Let's say you're spending five hours a week doing tasks you could delegate to a VA. Obviously, hiring that VA resource frees up five hours of your time every week! Let's take that a step further.

That's five additional hours every week you can devote to sales. Are you following me so far?

Many business owners say "I can't afford it." Well, in a scenario like I've just outlined, I would argue you can't afford **not** to hire a VA! (Apologies to my amazing middle school English teacher, Miss Monaco, for the double-negative – she's probably rolling over in her grave.)

Let me explain:

Hiring the VA frees up 260 hours of your time each year (5 hours per week * 52 weeks per year). How many sales can you achieve in 260 hours? Let's suppose each sale takes 4 hours of your time and is worth $1k in revenue. On average, that equates to $65k of additional sales (260 hours / 4 hours per sale * $1k per sale)!

"Well, you paint a rosy picture, Mr. Biz, but you forgot a critical piece of the puzzle – I still have to pay for the VA!"

Fair enough.

The cost for the VA? At $25 per hour for 260 hours, your VA cost is $6,500!

Can you afford to spend $6,500 for an incremental $65,000 in sales each year? (Sarcasm just might be my finest attribute – ask Mrs. Biz.) That's a 10x return on your investment! Mr. 10X, Grant Cardone, would be proud!

Tell me again about how you can't afford a VA? I'm waiting. I admit – sometimes my sarcasm is over-the-top. Not trying to be difficult – just trying to get you thinking outside of the box!

Hopefully, this chapter has demonstrated several examples, including "The Big Four", when, despite Mr. Biz's penchant for saving money, it does **<u>not</u>** make sense to DIY your business!

Chapter 7

HOW CAN YOUR COMPANY BE MORE EFFICIENT

In this chapter, we're going to discuss how to improve efficiency in your business. Granted, this is going to be a bit difficult to do efficiently – pun intended. Clearly, it is going to be different in every different type of business and niche, etc., but there are still some overarching themes we can go review that pertain to most every type of business. That being said, you know I like my statistics. It has been estimated that inefficiency can cost the average business 20-30% of their revenue[14].

Think about that for a second . . .

Suppose you have a $1 million revenue business . . . that means you could be wasting $300k from inefficiency!! Holy crap!! OK – you might be saying there is now way in Hades that is accurate for your business. Fine. Let's suppose the people who calculated that estimate are off their rocker and inefficiency *only* costs your

---

[14] https://www.entrepreneur.com/article/286084

business 10% of revenue . . . that's still $100k!! I don't know about you but I would love to save $100k in waste in my business. If so, keep reading. If not, please invite me to your private island villa. Mr. Biz would love a killer vacation destination!

You're not necessarily going to be able to get rid of *all* of the inefficiency in your business. There are certain things you can't just "get rid of", but I'm fairly certain you can improve upon it to a large extent.

Definitely control your waste, which is a big part of inefficiency. I know that's a giant "DUH!". However, what typically occurs is business owners settle into complacency and they don't consider potential areas in which they have waste. Too often it becomes the good ole – "this is how we've always done it" mentality. You've heard me say this before but if you're not raising the bar each year, you're falling behind because, I promise you, at least some of your competitors are!

When you cut costs by reducing waste, it allows you to focus on the big picture stuff: innovating and improving. You don't have resources to do that if you're always putting out fires – i.e. you're inefficient. You become too reactive and limit your ability to be proactive. That's not a position in which we want to be. While that seems obvious, I can attest that it happens regularly. In the day-to-day hustle and bustle, it is tough to remember to pull your head out of the proverbial weeds. And, sometimes, you think you are doing this . . . but, alas, you aren't. You need the correct mindset to do so.

Aside from focusing intently on waste, you need to assess your current productivity. Every business should measure their productivity in some form or fashion. This is not a "nice to have"; it is a necessity. Develop a list of Key Performance Indicators (KPIs) that you review each and every month. Of course, these KPIs will be different for every business.

Think of the crucial pieces of your business. What drives your revenue? What are your largest expenses? Then, break those down into what is most pertinent for you. Maybe one KPI is how many widgets your workers produce per hour? Whatever they are, track them, share them with workers who impact them and constantly strive to improve them. Don't forget to brainstorm with your team – they are in the trenches and often have great ideas. You only improve what you measure!

One additional comment on KPIs – once you discover the bounty they can bring, you can get KPI-crazy. Guard against that. I recommend having no more than five primary KPIs upon which you are focusing at a given time. Over time, those five KPIs will change. If you throw ten different measures at your team, they will be overwhelmed (as will you) and nothing will get accomplished. It is much better to have laser focus on five at a time. Once any of them reach the goal level, move them to another report for management only so they will still be monitored but won't be the focus by your frontline employees. If they falter, move them back into the top five until you get them back in order.

I recommend only five in focus at a time for several reasons but especially considering a common example most can relate to – weight loss/getting in better shape. Many people fail with this, not because they are lazy, but more likely because they become overwhelmed:

- Cut your calories
- Don't eat carbs
- Get to the gym 5 times every week
- Eliminate sugar
- Do cardio 4 times per week
- Drink 1 gallon of water each day
- No more soda
- No more alcohol
- Increase your fiber intake
- Do 4 sets of 15 reps of every exercise
- Take your recommended 12 vitamins every day
- Don't eat past 9PM
- Eat healthy fats
- Do at least 10 exercises per workout
- Get 8 hours of sleep every day
- Don't even LOOK at a dessert
- Etc.

People try to do all of this, all at the same time! It's no wonder many fail!

By the way, anyone who skipped down until they saw the above bullets is probably thoroughly confused – "What in THE heck do these bullet points have to do with improving efficiency in my business??" ☉

When I was a personal trainer, I would initially have clients focus on only three things for thirty straight days. Once they had one of them down for thirty days, we would add another and repeat the cycle. You needed thirty consecutive successful days before you add more.

This is exactly the same concept with your business. Narrow your KPI focus for impact. In this case, more is *not* better. If you want impact, do not inundate your team! Otherwise, nothing gets done and your business remains "fat".

For example, if you have a service business – lawn care, HVAC, plumbing, janitorial, electrical, etc. – one of the key things I look at is billable hours from your production employees. If you have a service business and you don't track this, you could be at that 30% inefficiency mentioned. Seriously, please-please-please begin tracking this KPI today! You will likely be shocked by the results. The reason it is so powerful is it measures the effectiveness of your production labor expense.

Joe the technician, who you're paying for an 8-hour day – how many of those 8 hours are you billing to customers? Whatever the answer, it speaks volumes. After all, if you are making double your employee's hourly wage, you should be in good shape, right?

Consider this simple example:

- You bill your labor at 200% - meaning you charge the customer double the hourly rate
- You pay Joe $20 per hour
- Because of schedule that isn't full, travel time, etc. – he logs 4 billable hours per day
- You pay him $160 per day (+ benefits?) – 8 hours * $20/hour
- His billable hours (aside from product) earn $160 – 4 hours * $40/hour
- $160 earned - $160 paid = $0, or break-even, right?
- Nope! This doesn't account for your overhead expenses!

- In this scenario, having Joe as an employee is actually a losing proposition!
- Say what?! (Sorry, Joe)

This is the type of eye-opening information that can come from measuring your billable hours. I once worked with a business that when we started tracking their billable hours we found they were at rate of around 50%. Put another way – they were paying their guys for 8 hours but each only had 4 billable hours every day (like the above example). You can imagine that was not profitable. Once we began tracking and monitoring, it steadily rose and they are currently sitting at ~82%! That is pretty solid.

Getting to 100% is utopia but almost impossible. However, your target level is what you need to reflect in your pricing. Pricing is a whole other ball of wax, of course! There are a multitude of ways to improve this KPI. But first, you have to actually track and monitor it in order to make improvements! I can assure you – once you begin tracking it and sharing the results with your team, it **will** improve. Your employees will know it is important to you so they will be mindful of it. You will watch it like a hawk to look for ways to improve it. Finally, amongst your employees, no one wants to rank low in something that is important to their boss, right?

As mentioned, before you get too crazy, for the most part getting to 100% is going to be almost impossible to accomplish, especially with travel time involved. If you charge for travel time in some way, then you can get closer to 100%. Of course, there are different ways to incorporate that but most businesses have moved away from that in the service industries.

OK – enough on billable hours! If I have not adequately conveyed yet, it is critically important for every service business that bills by the hour.

What else is important for efficiency?

Consider every possible productivity measure in your measure, then narrow down your initial list to those that have the highest impact on expenses. If you're in manufacturing, you have a whole slew of different things you need to consider as far as how long it takes to produce a widget, how much raw material goes into each widget, productivity per employee, waste per widget, percentage of widgets produced that don't meet quality standards, etc.

In the food industry, some key measures are: what is the spoilage rate? What percentage of what you produce has to be redone because it wasn't done accurately or the quality was poor? Cost per unit of each product? Table turns per hour? Sales per customer? Sales per staff cost per hour? Things like that.

Every business is different, but if you have a repair or install business, consider this often-overlooked measure: how often do you have to go back out to a job site to correct an issue – quality, install, or otherwise? That is a killer for efficiency and profitability. First of all, just to leave the shop – there and back – that is time you're paying for, but is most likely not billable. Therefore, it is costing your company money but not earning revenue. Further, that is time your employees could be doing other things – doing other installs or producing additional product. This productivity drag could also delay other deliveries, thereby impacting customer service! It has a negative domino effect. That makes it difficult to manage the current schedule; it has created *another* inefficiency.

For other KPIs, consider what other pieces that move the needle for your business. That will give you another idea as to where to start for your initial list of five. Another idea is to look at your expenses. Start with what drives the highest expense lines. How can you measure what drives those lines? More than likely that's where you have the most opportunity to improve. In a lot of businesses, that's going to be either raw materials (manufacturing), or more likely, it's employee expense.

As I alluded to earlier, when you target these inefficiencies, they will improve. As that occurs and they become strengths, target others that are now the lowest hanging fruit on the inefficiency tree. Every time you resolve an inefficiency, look for the next one, starting with the most impactful.

Identify each and put together an action plan. From there, regularly monitor your progress. Depending on the measure, you might be monitoring it weekly. At a minimum, check progress each month. Take the time to sit down and review the key aspects you identified and make sure you're making progress towards becoming more efficient.

If I received a quarter every time I said the word "efficiency", I'd be rich by the end of this chapter.

Monitoring and accountability are key. With most businesses I work with, every month we review an overall package:

- Balance sheet review

- Income statement Current vs. Prior Year

- Income statement Current vs. Budget

- KPIs Current vs. Goal

Depending on the business, there are other reports in the package but this the minimum.

How are we trending? If we are kicking butt, let's determine why, so we can amplify that and continue improving. If we are slipping, let's determine why, so we can right the ship. Bottom line, what changes do we need to make to reach our goals? This sounds obvious and simple, yet the sheer act of reviewing each month and not shying away from the tough conversations, when necessary, will propel your business. I promise you that. Do you do that now? If not, please institute it asap.

Up next, you want to make it as easy as possible for employees to efficiently do their jobs. Much of that simply boils down to transparent communication. Most employees want to perform well and please their boss. Therefore, if they know what is important to you, they will be sure they are hitting their marks on those things.

Along the lines of communication, always listen to your employees. After filtering through some of the possible whiner commentary or gossip (there is some of this in every company – it isn't just your employees), you will be pleasantly surprised with their suggestions.

Side note – you can nip the whining and gossip in the bud with the proper response. If they know you don't like or tolerate it, for the most part, they won't give it. When our kids were small and they would start whining, I would tell them they needed to go to their room if they were going to whine because it hurt my ears. Worked every time! Clearly, you can't treat your employees like children. I'm not suggesting that – just illustrating a point.

However, in order to foster those suggestions, you need to create the proper environment. If they feel like you never listen, they won't say anything. You have to be honest with yourself about how receptive you are to employee suggestions. Especially in situations where you are no longer in the field, you need to be willing to listen to possible new approaches.

My recommendation to help with this . . .

As long as it is not complaining or gossip, EVERY TIME an employee makes a suggestion, reply positively, even if you don't like the idea. "Wow! Thanks, Barb. I've never thought of that! Let me think about how that might work." Employees love receiving positive feedback from their boss. That type of response will encourage them to offer future suggestions. Just like all of us, every idea we come up with isn't always the best. However, consider this – if that employee offers five ideas and you implement two of them that save you 5% each . . . that's a 10% savings! But, if you react negatively to their first idea, you shut them down and never get to hear their other four ideas.

That being said, make sure if you do not implement their idea, you follow-up with every suggestion. You don't have to provide a detailed explanation. Something simple is best. That way you avoid sounding negative.

"Thanks again for your suggestion. We took a look at the impact it had on the overall business and, while it helped production by 4%, it had a 7% detrimental impact on the front office. For that reason, we did not implement it. However, I love your way of thinking! Keep those ideas coming!"

More than likely, they only considered their piece of the business and didn't recognize the negative impact on another part of the company. A great way to solicit ideas from employees? Very simple, yet massively effective . . .

"If you ran this company for a day, what would you do differently?"

Of course, you are bound to get some of this –

"I would fire Jerry! He is lazy!"

However, in general, the positives outweigh the negatives. In addition, this type of question boosts morale. Your employees see you not only want their input, but you trust their opinion. They most likely look up to you as the "smart one" but here you are asking their opinion! You are showing vulnerability and trust. Super powerful.

Heck – if you really want to drive efficiency, let's take this a step further. Aligning with the Mr. Biz pro-performance incentive stance – you can offer incentives for implemented ideas. To streamline the process, you might provide a suggestion box in which employees can suggest changes to improve the business. If their idea is implemented, you will give them a bonus that equates to 10-20% of the annual financial impact of the idea.

Taking it a step further 2.0, increase retention by paying out that bonus based on actual results, not just projections.

In addition, when employees see this in action and hear about payouts, it has a few positive impacts:

- Encourages additional improvement suggestions – others want a piece of the pie

- Improves morale – they see it actually *does* pay off, not just management hot air

- Increases trust – they see you **do** want their opinion

- Increases retention – people want to work where they are appreciated

Think about your own work experience if you haven't always been an owner. How many times in the past have you caught yourself saying something like this?

- "If I ran this place, we would definitely do/not do . . ."
- "Why do they make us do 'xyz'?"
- "We should be doing/not doing . . ."

If so, you, yourself, had improvement suggestions to make! Hopefully, your open suggestion environment also improves morale in this sense – suppose an employee has one of the aforementioned complaints and airs it to a co-worker. However, the co-worker knows your receptiveness to suggestions and says – "Hey, that's a great idea! You should submit it to the suggestion box. If not, keep quiet. At this company, you have an opportunity to express ideas. If you choose not to do so, that's on you."

Think about how much angst this type of environment can squash. You are, literally, telling them – if you have a complaint/suggestion, let us know. They can get it off their chest – anonymously or not. As mentioned, you will get your fair share of drama-type issues, for sure. But sifting through those to the good ones can prove to be beneficial on multiple fronts.

OK – so maybe you don't have a field-based service company. Maybe you have an office-based service company – a law firm, a consulting firm, financial advisory, etc.

Here is a telling statistic: e-mail takes up 28% of an employee's time[15]. Plus, the average person takes 23 minutes to get fully back on task after an interruption. How many times each day are you interrupted by checking email? Wait – what?? Most office-based businesses are probably not surprised to hear that, but it's just crazy how much it is.

"How can your office-based service business save $151k per year?"

Consider this:

If your office-based employee makes $100k per year, presuming a salaried approach, they cost you $48 per hour (salary only). That means they are spending $108 per day on emails. Now, granted, in this scenario, a decent chunk of their email time is spent answering client questions and the like. And, depending on your business model, some of that might include billable time.

---

[15] https://frontapp.com/blog/2018/07/20/how-much-time-are-you-spending-on-email/

However, let's suppose even just 1/3 of their time on email is not business related. What impact is that? Are you ready for this? That's almost $9k per $100k employee!

Quick and simple scenario of an office-based service firm:

- 2 employees at $300k salary
- 1 employee at $200k salary
- 4 employees at $100k salary
- 3 employees at $50k salary

This is a 10-person office-based service business – maybe a law firm, for example.

What would you guess the financial/inefficiency impact is of 1/3 of the 28% email time being personal in nature?

How about ~$151k every year?!

Now I'm not suggesting employees can't have personal emails. In today's day and age, that is unrealistic. Having a Draconian policy for that is sure to decrease retention. However, what if we reduced the personal portion of 28% email time from 33% to 10%. How much efficiency in the form of dollars, would that save us? In this example, $97k!

Again, we aren't saying you can't have personal email; we're saying limit it to 10% of your email time. That demonstrates empathy, reasonableness and potentially saves $97k in lost productivity each year. How about that for an impact on efficiency?!

Another way to handle email more efficiently – try to have designated times each day when you check email. Other than that, keep your email closed so you are not constantly interrupted with notifications. This way you limit the number of interruptions each day.

With an office environment and email inefficiency, here's another idea . . . I will sound like "Old Man Biz" . . . pick up the phone and make a call vs. trading 12 emails back & forth. Crazy idea, I know. Eliminate communication barriers or hurdles to increase efficiency.

OK – back to field-based service businesses . . .

If you have any type of field business where you're traveling to customers, you definitely want to look at your travel time and how can you streamline it. Of course, if you only have one tech/crew, you are mostly stuck on this one. However, even with just two techs/crews, there are efficiencies to be had. For example, depending on where they live, team 1 handles the west half of the area and team 2 handles the east half of the area. Definitely consider breaking your crews up geographically to reduce travel time. As mentioned earlier, travel time is most likely wasted time – you are paying your team but not earning revenue for it. That equates to inefficiency.

While you may be thinking that is minimal, I can tell you – the cumulative impact is massive! Here is another quick example to illustrate the potential savings:

- 3 crews with 2 employees each
- Each crew could save 1.5 hours of travel time each day, if managed better
- Combined hourly wage (with benefits) per crew is $50
- Aside from the lower mileage and vehicle wear & tear . . .

- Saving 1.5 hours per day travel time per crew = $67.5k per year!
- $67.5k = an extra employee @ $32.45/hr
- How much annual revenue is that?

Imagine the impact if you have a bigger operation!

During this final section, let's focus on some electronic/digital solutions. Primarily, this means automation – how effective can that be if you have a manufacturing company. I worked with one company that had been in business for about 30 years and some of the equipment they had was old and antiquated. As you can imagine, with the innovations that have taken place over the last 30 years… the efficiency difference was staggering! Of course, there are some capital costs involved with getting up-to-date equipment. We did a cost-benefit analysis on it and it was a no-brainer.

When you're in the weeds of your business and managing it day-to-day, this is one of those things you might not necessarily consider.

- Is your equipment antiquated?

- What is the cost of new equipment?

- How about used equipment?

- What is the productivity increase for new equipment?

- How do those compare to the ongoing expense?

- For how much can you sell your existing equipment?

- Can you lease new equipment?

All of these should be considered when evaluating your options. If you are unsure, reach out to an expert. Making a good decision in this instance can make a big difference for your company.

Another thing I'll talk about here, and this is a little bit more specific and would have more of an impact on some businesses vs. others, but consider your energy management – your heating and cooling. Review your energy management process, and even aside from helping the environment, you can also save a ton of money.

We recently had a guest on my radio show, Bruce Ostermeyer, and he talked about telecom and all the different ways you can save money with that. It's not just energy, but that does save money and improve efficiency. A simple item like having a programmed thermostat in your office during the summer will help to be more energy efficient.

Let's say you're a West Coast business and it's warm year-round. You don't necessarily need to be running your air conditioning 24 hours a day. That just wastes electricity.

When you see how much money you can save:

- If you're cooling 5,000 square feet of space
- After hours, you turn your thermostat up 10 degrees
- Then next the morning you have it kick on a half-hour before everyone arrives, to lower temperature, so it's all nice and cool by the time people get into the office.

I'll tell you, that alone makes a *huge* difference. We have a programmable thermostat in our house and I know the difference it makes just in our house, which is not a giant warehouse.

Things like that are easy, low hanging fruit. You should look at your water consumption as well. The ways you can repurpose water, like potable vs. non-potable, if you're a manufacturing company, can save money. And you're doing your part to help the environment. Obviously, that's a good thing.

It's difficult discussing all of these options with different businesses in mind, because some of these items are more applicable than others, but hopefully you were able to glean a few nuggets and found some value in this chapter.

Chapter 8

HIRE THE BEST . . . FASTER!

In this chapter, as the title suggests, we're going to talk about how to hire better people faster. Expediting this process and ensuring you get good people is critical for growth and success! We're going to learn how to recruit with the best methods and sources. After we get through recruiting, we're going to dive into the hiring process.

So, how do you make that process better? How do you ensure you get good people and make the process efficient? What I mean by that is, if you've got an opening, you shouldn't have to interview 15 people to fill it! That is completely inefficient and a waste of your time. Who has time to interview 15 people? If you have to interview 15 people to hire for 1 opening, then your process is broken.

It's not the candidate's fault – it's the way you are recruiting people that's not efficient. Maybe your job descriptions are, shall we say, less than optimal? Maybe they don't do a good job of outlining exactly what the job entails, so you attract a poor slate of candidates? We will cover things to improve your process.

A lot of service businesses I have worked with use Craigslist to source candidates. My take on that approach? I think that is "so 2012"! Haha. I think that source worked much better in years past but not so much any longer. In my post-2015 experience, Craigslist will produce a boatload of . . . crappy candidates! That just leads to the previously mentioned scenario of needing to interview 15 people for 1 opening – not good.

Let's talk about a few other free resources that might be more fruitful for you. One of them is tapping into your network! This is effective because you are receiving candidates that have a built-in recommendation from a known source, not just some random person off the street. If someone you already know and trust refers someone to you, don't you automatically feel more comfortable with that candidate? You should! Taking that further, that person likely already has interest because of the mutual connection. That mutual connection probably gave them some information about you, about your company, your culture, how you roll, etc. Hopefully people you know and trust are not going to send you people that they wouldn't hire themselves.

If you think about it, just as you recommend folks for anything, you've already recognized a possible good match. I mean, I recommend people all of the time. If I refer you and you have a bad experience, that's a bad reflection on me. I think most people look at referrals that way.

Here's another one right under your nose . . .

Ask your employees!

This is even better because your employees have first-hand knowledge of your company culture, how you do business, what the job entails, etc. In the first example I mentioned with your network – your friends might not do business with you but they know what type of person you are. However, they don't know what it's like to work *for* you. Presuming you treat your employees well, they can be supreme recruiters and advocates for you to find good people.

Here's another point in your favor with utilizing employee referrals . . . Employees have a vested interest in bringing other good employees to your company. They don't want to bring in crappy employees because then they will have to pick up the slack, right? They will avoid that and bring you good people. It's almost like a very good pre-screening. Your employees weed out bad candidates (by not recommending them) before they even get to you. The employee referral candidates walk in the door with a good understanding of the lay of the land. That relieves you of needing to interview 15 people to find 1 good candidate.

To further encourage employee referrals, you can even offer a bonus for referrals that get hired and successfully make it through their probationary period. That gives your people a little more incentive to make sure they are keeping an eye out for qualified folks.

Somewhat related to that – when you ask employees to spread the word, suggest they share it on their social media accounts, such as Facebook. We have all seen the power of social media in some form or another. Tap into that and use it!

If you don't have one already (you should), start a Facebook page for your business. Share your opening on your business page as well. That makes it even easier for your employees to share it in their network.

While you're in the Facebook world, don't forget to post it on local business or networking group pages. They are easy to find and your post can get in front of a lot of eyes with them. And . . . they're free!!

To demonstrate how powerful social media can be: let's say you have 10 employees who each have 300 friends on Facebook; each of them share it on their profile; you have just *potentially* reached 10 x 300, or 3,000 people. Then, if anyone in their reach engages with it, that possibly exposes it to much of their network as well. It can quickly reach a large swath of people and the best part of that? It's free! Take advantage of that.

Make sure you're visible wherever your candidates are. Where are your optimal candidates? Make sure you're *there*. If you're in the service industry, where do people in your industry go; where are they going to see your job description or your ad? I had a client that had warehouse openings that required a lot of physical activity. We put the job description in every gym within a 20-mile radius. We received a flood of applications and almost all passed the initial screening because they were physically able to perform the job. They were visible where their candidates were!

You can also consider a paid recruiting source. For example, you can use ZipRecruiter or Indeed. Those are two that are very popular and, in some cases, effective right now. You can usually get pretty decent results with either, depending on your business, of course. Both offer a service that's a decent value in most cases. They enable you to hit your target audience reasonably well.

Another angle I love to use that is free is utilize local public organizations. It could be a local college – maybe you need an intern, maybe you need young people to work part-time schedules, maybe you can target graduating seniors for permanent jobs. Don't forget vocational trade schools. They can be an outstanding source for many service businesses. Let's say you have an auto repair shop – geez, that would be fertile ground to find really good people. You can also go to government agencies like an economic development agency or a Chamber of Commerce.

Here's an out-of-the-box idea

We used this at business with warehouse manufacturing jobs. We targeted halfway houses that were on the bus route between the house and our warehouse. The owner was willing to give these people a second chance. He put a couple stipulations in place to weed out possible issues with which he didn't want to deal – no drug or violence convictions.

This one comes from my heart. I'm a Board member and Treasurer for a nonprofit called *Family Promise.* We help homeless families get back on their feet and sometimes that's in the form of helping them find a job. So, definitely consider registering with similar nonprofit agencies in your area. If you hire people through an organization such as *Family Promise,* you are helping people get back on their feet *and* you can find good, eager candidates.

Here's one I love, but it is often overlooked – add an employment application form to your website. That can help keep your pipeline active for when you do have an opening. With these candidates, you at least know they are interested in working for you because they went through the trouble of finding your website and completing the application. This also gives you a place to send people who are interested in working in your company.

I know you've seen these lots of times on semi-trucks: "Now Hiring" signs with a phone number or website. Put those signs on *your* vehicles. However, send them to your website, not a phone number. Handling a bunch of random "are you hiring?" phone calls is time-consuming and unnecessarily takes you away from helping your customers or booking new appointments. This is another reason why having an employment application on your website is helpful.

If you have a service business, you've got vehicles with branding logos and the like on them (if you don't, shame on you!). Another item you definitely should add is a "Now Hiring" sign. Put that signage in a less "prime" spot, but don't skip it. You will be surprised what you receive from it. Granted, about half of them will be a whole bunch of craziness but the other half will be reasonable candidates to consider.

If you are in the service business, you know the workers are very transient and, consequently, they communicate with each other often. As I always say – make it easy for people to do business with you. In this case, that equates to making it easy for prospective candidates to apply to work with you. The two things you can do to facilitate that are the online application and signage on your vehicles. Especially since you are a preferred employer (you are, right?), you want to make it easy for the 'Rock Star' employees to reach you!

The last recruiting tip I want to mention, and it is sort of on the hiring side, really, so it's a good segue-way between the two: When someone leaves and you have an opening, don't just automatically post the job and rush to hire someone. First, be honest with yourself and determine if you could make it work without replacing the position. Don't just hire someone for the sake of filling the position. There are several items to consider:

A) Does this position directly impact revenue?

B) Does this position directly impact customer service?

C) AND, are you heading into your slow season?

If A or B are true, you should continue down your hiring journey. You don't want to "upset the apple cart" with either of those items. If you're being honest with yourself, both of those options will pay for themselves in short order so it makes financial sense to fill the position. If C is true, it doesn't necessarily mean to not fill the position. In that situation, you should consider delaying the hiring so you don't carry that salary through the slow season. Strive to time your hiring so your new employee has adequate training time to get up to speed prior to busy season beginning.

Those options aside – do you *really* need to hire that position? If it doesn't directly impact revenue or customer service, take a hard look. Can you shuffle things around and make it work without filling it, even if just temporarily? When I say "make it work", I don't mean struggle through and make your other employees work mega hours and burn them out. Oftentimes, though, we don't ask ourselves these tough questions and, consequently, we waste money.

Sometimes we get into "this is the way we've always done it mode"- someone leaves so you need to hire a replacement. But maybe your business has changed and there are better options than just automatically hiring that position? Consider this one: maybe you **do** need to hire someone, but not for those same tasks?

I used this mentality in my CFO roles in the corporate world. We would have departments that lost people and the jobs would be open for 90-120 days. I regularly reviewed the aging of our open positions. For those in the 90+ day range, the conversation would go something like this:

Me: "Do we really need to fill this position?"

Hiring manager: "Oh yeah, we absolutely need to fill it. We can't survive without it."

Me: "Well, then how the heck have we been surviving for the last 90+ days without it?"

Before you think I'm a complete jerk . . .

Yes, there were times when we had "survived" because other employees stepped up and busted their butts to fill the void. As a result, they were approaching burn-out, which is not a good thing. I recognize that scenario and I'm not suggesting that's the way to go. However, in my experience, we, more often than not, fall into the "if someone leaves, we automatically replace them" mindset. As your business grows and changes, this is especially important to consider.

I'll give you a simple example:

Let's say you recently purchased new software that significantly streamlined several admin tasks in your business. Then, a person in an admin position resigns. In that situation, maybe you don't need to replace that admin position because the new software increased efficiency to the point where that position is no longer needed. However, not so fast my friend – maybe you can re-allocate those salary dollars to a sales position to increase revenue? (See, I'm not always a "meanie".)

Another angle to consider is hiring virtual help or even a temporary employee, *especially* if it's just to fill a seasonal need. There is no need to take on salary and benefits until/unless it makes financial sense for the full year. Of course, if you hire a short-term resource, you will pay a premium in the short term but you will save money in the long run vs. hiring a full-time employee. Heck, for most seasonal businesses, this is a fantastic option! Owners tend to think too narrowly. They don't always consider all options available to them. Sometimes that is a product of them being stretched too thin and wearing too many hats.

Another financial benefit is if you hire a temporary employee, you don't have to pay for employee benefits. Also, if you ever do have a permanent opening, a temporary employee you have worked with provides a pipeline to a good employee that already knows your business.

This is yet another recruiting tool! What better indication do you need than actual job performance? It really doesn't get any better than that!

Let's jump into the actual hiring process.

The first thing I want to lead with on the hiring side is a big one:

Hire based on loyalty, work ethic and character; everything else can be learned!

If you find someone with those three characteristics, hire them immediately! So many times when we hire people, we look intently for technical skills. Of course, depending on their role in your business, those *are* important – but it shouldn't just be that. How many times have you hired someone with really good technical skills, but they severely lacked one of these three intangibles? How did that work out for you? Think about it for a second. I'm willing to bet you're having an "a-ha" moment right now! No worries – that's why you're reading this book, right?

Those hires often end up being terrible employees. People don't like working with them; they're not coachable, etc. I promise you – this is based on many years of experience and hiring hundreds of people – if you hire based on those three traits, it is difficult to fail.

Another thing to do is make sure you are a viable employer – build your employer brand. Sounds simple enough, right? Here's a statistic on this for you:

73% of candidates are passive job seekers[16]

They're not currently looking for a new job, **but** they are open to new opportunities. So, make sure you're a 'preferred' employer in your local market in your industry. By the way, before you get too excited about 73%, keep in mind that could include your employees as well!

Here's another stat to consider:

84% of job seekers say reputation of the company is important[17]

For example, be sure you respond to online engagement. – reviews, comments, etc. Doing so shows you are an action-oriented business. In turn, that helps you become a preferred employer in your niche. When that happens, recruiting and hiring becomes easy. Candidates will come to you! You will have a steady pipeline of candidates from which to choose. That enables you to be more selective when hiring.

In my corporate days, Goldman Sachs was **the** place to be for investment banking. They worked long and hard to make their brand the place to be for aspiring investment bankers. They would have 1,000+ strong candidates for every opening! That creates an entirely new set of hiring challenges but we won't concern ourselves with those for now.

---

[16] https://www.talentnow.com/recruitment-statistics-2018-trends-insights-hiring-talented-candidates/

[17] https://www.talentnow.com/recruitment-statistics-2018-trends-insights-hiring-talented-candidates/

Here's more motivation to make your hiring process as efficient as possible – be decisive! The best candidates are off the market in about 10 days[18]. That's it! If you take too long interviewing and/or making a decision, more often than not, you will miss out on the primo candidates. If, for some reason, your process gets delayed, communication is key. Make sure you are reaching out to them in a timely manner. Do what you say you're going to do, when you say you're going to do it. Delays and lack of communication are frustrating for candidates. Have you ever been on the receiving end of either of those? If so, didn't it make you want to pull your hair out? At the interview:

"We will reach out to you within a week with our decision."

Two weeks later and you've heard nothing! In the meantime, if you are a top candidate, you are likely entertaining offers from other companies that <u>**do**</u> have their hiring process in order.

This is one of the things I think helped me acquire the best talent when I was in the corporate world. After going through the rigorous review of whether we needed to re-fill the position, I ran a tight ship for hiring. We would assemble a hiring team with each member having specific duties –

- Who screened resumes
- Who scheduled the interviews
- Who performed the interviews
- Who weighed-in on the hiring decision
- Who weighed-in on the offer

---

[18] https://www.talentnow.com/recruitment-statistics-2018-trends-insights-hiring-talented-candidates/

- Who officially made the offer

Even further, I liked to schedule the interviews in tight bunches to make it as efficient as possible. Optimally, we might have four interviewers simultaneously interviewing four candidates. Then, at the conclusion of the four interviews, all four interviewers would immediately meet to discuss the candidates while they were fresh in our minds. It didn't always work out this uniformly, but when it did, it was a thing of beauty. We could run these interviews on a Friday, then the final decision maker could take the weekend to think it over (if needed) and we could make an offer on Monday – BOOM!

Because we had a robust pre-screening process, we could almost always make a choice among our slate of candidates. If not, we might bring two of them back for additional interviews with another 1-2 interviewers to ensure we were making the best decision. Further, sometimes the decision was – none of the four are good enough. In that case, we would kick into Plan B and start the ball rolling to bring in another slate of candidates in the same manner. Because of our diligent selection process upfront, the latter two scenarios rarely occurred.

Use military-like precision with your hiring process and it will pay huge dividends! The process will be faster; it will be efficient; you won't lose out on the best candidates; and you will have less disruption due to an open position in your business. All good things.

By the way, a streamlined hiring process will also benefit you and, more importantly, your existing team members. The last thing you need when you're already down a key position is to lose another position because that person is frustrated by the delay in bringing on a new resource. That just negatively compounds the situation!

Here's another obvious, yet often overlooked, tip for hiring:

Make sure your job description is as accurate as possible, including the less glamorous responsibilities of the job

As I often say to our girls – "Life is about expectations". Employers often try to "dress up" a job to make it seem more glamorous to candidates. Then, once that person starts, they suffer from the dreaded, "I didn't sign up for this crap!" situation. That leaves you with an unhappy new employee and an unhappy boss because that new employee is not performing well. Neither works for you.

You need to be completely transparent with candidates, including the 'warts' of the job. Otherwise, in reality you're just selling them a bill of goods to get them onboard, which *will* bite you in the rear end. You will likely end up frustrated with their performance and they will likely quit from their frustration. Again, if you're hiring the best people, bear in mind that while they were seeking employment, they probably had other offers or options at their disposal. Sure, they chose your company then, but all it takes is a phone call to re-ignite that fire with a prior option. As is always true and a wise man once said –

"Honesty is the best policy"

Want to "dress up" your job description to candidates in a way that is fair to them and helps you recruit the best? Simple. Highlight what makes working at *your* company better than competitors. If you're a plumbing company, don't just include the typical things a plumber would do in your business. Every plumbing company does that right – Every. Single. One. You need to show people why they *want* to work at John Doe Plumbing.

Each potential hire is likely, at some point, to ask themselves the following question –

"Why should I leave where I'm at?"

If you can't provide a compelling reason, then you probably won't be able to attract top talent. I'm not being harsh. It's just that simple. You can't just always over-pay to attract people. That will most likely work in the short term. However, money or not, if they don't like working for you, they **will** leave! You heard it here first – mark it down. Best-case: if they don't leave, they will be a disruptive employee (otherwise known as a PITA – Pain In The A$$) and drag down morale for your remaining team members. Mark my words – 1 of those 2 scenarios will play out before your eyes and it won't be good.

Let's just be honest – at the end of the day, attracting talented, new employees isn't a whole lot different than the marketing you do to attract new customers. Let that sink in for a minute . . . am I wrong?

I don't mean cheesy, sales-guy marketing. I mean you need to demonstrate to customers/prospective new employees why they should do business with you/they should join your team. It all boils down to the same thing, right? Value!

Consider this scenario:

Someone is a little bit disgruntled in their current job, but not necessarily actively seeking another job. They're passive, but they're willing to consider new opportunities. By putting something in your job description that is compelling (read: being a preferred employer) and gives them a reason to consider working for you vs. their current employer, you open the proverbial door. Without it, they keep chugging along where they are without a second thought.

Now you might be saying – "That sounds great, Mr. Biz, but . . . what are those 'compelling' things that turn heads?"

Look, I have a great deal of experience but you can probably answer that better than me if you give it some thought. Here's a good starting point – consider these two questions:

1) What is it like working at a competitor?

2) What do employees in my industry want most?

Here is a quick example to get your wheels turning:

I worked with a salon owner. Of course, that industry is very transient so she suffered from poor retention. Other than paying more, which wasn't profitable over the long haul, she didn't know how to keep her people and attract new ones. We had a quick brainstorming session.

Considering the two questions above, we evaluated her current employees. She had 11 employees and 8 of them were single mothers. Single mothers seemed to be a pattern since 73% of her then-current team fell into that category. We considered what are the biggest challenges for single mothers. I will spare you the details and cut to the chase – we partnered with a daycare facility, that happened to be two doors down from the salon, to offer discounted daycare for employees. It was a win-win because salon employees could obtain less expensive, yet very good, daycare services for their children and the daycare knew they had a steady flow of children from the salon employee moms.

7 of the 8 single moms enrolled; 2 of the 3 non-single moms also enrolled! So, 9 of 11 employees were able to take advantage of the daycare benefit! Not only was it a cost-effective option but, obviously, it was convenient. Oh, and if that wasn't enough, Moms could visit their kids during their breaks! That is a quadruple win!

The cynics out there might say – "That's a great feel-good story but what about the business-related results?" Fair enough. How about this . . . prior to this change and despite her best efforts, her turnover rate was 36%. That means each year she lost (and had to replace) about 4 of her 11 employees. After implementing this idea (which, by the way, didn't cost her a dime), in 16 months thus far, she hasn't lost any employees – 0% turnover! Yes, 0%!

Moreover, because word travels fast, she has a waiting-list of possible replacements. So, if by chance, someone does leave, she has a pipeline of potential employees from which to choose. By implementing one simple change, her retention and revenue challenges have been solved! And, she became a preferred employer.

What else?

Don't forget to utilize social media – it is super powerful! You can use it to promote your company to be that 'active brand'. Also, use social media to check your candidates. You likely do a background check. Why not make a social media review part of your background check? As you can imagine, you can learn a lot about someone from their social media profile.

I'm not suggesting to stalk them for three hours on social media… you don't have to do that. However, as you likely know (but might not do), you can literally Google someone's name and find out a ton of information about them within 10 seconds.

I remember as a kid we would watch old re-runs of *"Leave it to Beaver"* every day, right before dinner (that definitely dates me but I assure you they were **old** re-runs). For those not familiar, there was a character that was friends with the two sons. In front of the parents, he was "Mr. Nice Guy", but he would *always* entice the boys into doing things they shouldn't be doing. His name was Eddie Haskell . . . I mention this goofy anecdote only because you're going to have some "Eddie Haskell" candidates. They're going to come in and interview, and you think they're great. Then, all of the sudden you go on their social media only to find out they've got something awful, whatever it might be. Point being, they're not the person you thought they were. Especially in today's day and age, once you narrow your search down to a couple of people and you're trying to decide which one to choose – go out and do a quick Google search on their name. That may help you make that final *and* better decision.

Another thing I want to mention is to make sure their personality fits. Again, that sounds obvious, but ensure it fits for several things:

If you need someone to be the face of your business:

- o Answer the phone;
- o Greet customers as they come through your front door;
- o If the candidate is passive and very shy – probably not a good fit
- o You want someone who is going to be bubbly and cheerful
- o Seek that personality trait
- o Not just that they have good skills with answering the phone or admin skills

Match their personality with the job. They will be happier when they arrive and they'll do a much better job for you. It makes all the difference in the world.

One final example I'll give you – I utilized this in the corporate world as well. When someone leaves, assess the team you currently have and determine what weaknesses are on the team.

You don't want to hire people that are just like you or just like everyone else on the team. In the scenario, you could end up with "group think" or a non-diverse skillset on your team. Hence, things don't get better because everyone thinks the same way, with mostly the same ideas. Or, you have skill gaps so you don't have expertise with certain tasks expected in your industry. You want to consider people with a different viewpoint.

I learned the importance of this in my corporate life. I had a boss and we went through the Myers-Briggs test, which, for those unfamiliar, is a personality test. All eight of us had the exact same personality type and he was really excited about that. I remember thinking – "That's not good because we all think the same way". You want to have some variety in there because it makes your team more well-rounded. That being said, it is proven that we seek to hire people that are like us. It's just what we do! However, you need to guard against that thinking.

A bonus tip and the last one I'll leave you with in this chapter is consider using a profit-sharing option that will position you above your competitors. We will talk more in-depth about how to best implement those in the 2nd volume of this book – "Pathway to *More* Profits".

By following these steps and tips, you will get the best of the best; the cream of the crop in your industry *and* you will get them on board much faster.

Chapter 9

BETTER PRICING & SERVICE FROM VENDORS

Every single business, whether you have a service business or a product-driven business, has vendors they use so this topic touches all of you. I don't think I've *ever* run into a person who doesn't have a vendor management horror story. During the sales process, when you're getting ready to sign a contract with the vendor, everything's rainbows and unicorns. Unfortunately, they sometimes seem to forget many of those promises. Let's talk through some of those situations and discuss how to avoid them.

Solid vendor management has to do with making it easy for people to do business with you, so being a good business partner for your vendors obviously makes all the difference in the world. By doing this, you create more of a win-win situation. The positive impact you can have on your business is tremendous. Most of you know this, but it crosses so many different lines.

I'm sure everyone has heard the expression, "You get what you pay for!". That is certainly true when it comes to selecting a vendor. Cost isn't always the best indicator of what vendor you should use. Don't choose a vendor solely based on price and definitely not because the sales person is nice. You might think I'm kidding but this happens often. People like to do business with people they like, of course. The sales person might be a great person but their product or service might stink!

Once you have a vendor, you want to foster that relationship into a strong partnership. Guess the best way to do that? Send them a card on their birthday? Maybe some cookies over the holidays? NOPE! Pay your bills on time! It is really that simple. Hold up your end of the bargain, so to speak.

Think about it as a business owner – how do you feel about late-paying customers? Unfortunately, we all have people who do not pay on time. Where do those customers "rank" with you? Not very high, I'm sure. [Side note: check out Chapter 3 to learn ways to minimize this burden]

If you're frequently late paying their invoices, how willing are they going to be to go the extra mile for you when you need it? As usual, it boils down to following the Golden Rule, right?

Let's say you have a dire situation where you *really* need to get a raw material or whatever they provide to you. You need it to expedite an order for one of your best customers. Are they going to bend over backwards to help you when you can't even pay them on time? Perfect example of how such a simple thing goes a long way in fostering a positive relationship.

Another important aspect to consider is to know the current marketplace. One part of that is to make sure you're not asking for something that's completely unreasonable. Let's say you have a vendor that does all your IT work. Expecting them to be at your business within two hours of reporting a problem is probably not a reasonable expectation (unless you pay a premium for that level of service). Of course, this is a prime example of where a Service Level Agreement (SLA) is key. More on that in a little bit . . .

Consider a situation where you have had a contract with a vendor for several years but the marketplace has changed and the level of service they are providing is no longer competitive. It could be the delivery or response time; it might be the cost. You're probably thinking – "Mr. Biz, that would never happen to me!" I can tell you with certainty it happens more often than you think. The primary reasons this occurs mostly boil down to four scenarios:

1) Signing a long-term contract without update provisions

2) Not performing an annual review of your contracts

3) Employing a "set-it-and-forget-it" attitude

4) Being too nice to your "buddy" who is taking advantage of you

So, my advice . . . well, duh – don't do any of those four things! Super helpful, right? Haha

#1 is easily rectified. If you are going to sign a long-term agreement with a vendor, ensure there are provisions that allow for appropriate changes, if the need arises. Otherwise, stick to short-term agreements.

#2 & #3 are closely related. You should be performing annual reviews of every contract or agreement you have in place. In fact, if your business is in a rapid growth phase, you should review them even more often. The primary reason being you may be able to negotiate more favorable terms based on a higher volume.

#4 is a bit touchy-feely, but important to consider. I have run into this in virtually every business with which I have worked. It makes sense. You are a nice person and want to give people the benefit of the doubt. It is our nature (most of us).

Feelings aside, always remember – you are running a business, not a charity. I completely understand you may develop close relationships with vendors, especially after doing business with them for several years. And, don't forget those suh-weet tickets he gave you for the Championship Game! However, again, you are running a business.

Schmoozing doesn't pay your bills

It is difficult to do sometimes but you need to strive to keep your professional relationship separate from the personal side. When in doubt, consider this: your vendor-owner buddy is also running a business. He knows **exactly** what it is like to sit in your seat. Don't feel bad about expecting him to meet his contractual obligations.

Can you cut your vendor buddy some slack every once in a while? Sure, why not? After all, he would do the same for you, right? "Ken, you just told me to follow the Golden Rule and I might want some slack from him at some point, so relax". That all may very well be true . . . but . . . unfortunately, there is more to it than that to consider.

Admittedly, this is the conservative/slightly paranoid side of me coming out, but this is something to at least keep in the back of your mind. Your generosity, in this case, could potentially come back to bite you in the butt. What? How?

What if you face the unfortunate situation of having to bring litigation action against a vendor for breaking their contract terms? And, because salespeople often float around to various companies within the industry, that vendor you're suing happens to know you allowed another supplier to break their terms and you *didn't* sue *them*?! Yeah, good luck with that one! In that scenario, by giving some slack, you took away legal leverage you have with other vendors. This isn't necessarily a common situation but it is something to keep in mind as you decide how to hold vendors accountable.

Believe me – if you discuss this with an attorney, they will make you paranoid enough to want to record every conversation or email you ever exchange with a vendor! I'm not suggesting that. It stinks, for sure, but, unfortunately, it is the litigious society in which we live.

By the way, you may be thinking: "My buddy, Bob, would *never* do that to me! Don't be so paranoid!" I'm here to tell you people (even "buddies") do funky things when it comes to impacting their financial situation. Heck, maybe something changed in their personal life and now they are scrambling. Who knows?

I will tell you – I have seen this tear apart families! When people face financial hardship, they often become desperate and make, what might seem like, irrational decisions. I'm not trying to make you ultra-paranoid. There is no need to hide your money under your mattress. **BUT** – I want you to be aware of what I have seen and how it could impact you.

Enough of the doom & gloom

Let's talk about other risks to consider with managing vendors.

In today's day & age, always consider privacy risks. It could be in the form of basic data (names & addresses of customers), patient or customer information (credit card numbers and/or medical history), intellectual property (your unique, but unprotected, approach/logo/slogan, etc.), prospect lists, etc. This is just off the top of my head; the list is almost endless. Think about all "private" information you or your customers would not want posted on the internet.

Some of the mentioned considerations are obvious, but also be mindful of others. Maybe your vendor regularly delivers to you and, therefore, has access to your warehouse. During those deliveries, do they see any "private"/proprietary processes or information that you would not want to be made public? Every cell phone is also a camera! Shoot – Mr. Delivery Guy might see something interesting during a delivery, then strategize to take pics or record a video during his next visit. Who knows?

Of course, the big thing nowadays is cyber security. That is an entire topic in and of itself, but do not neglect it with your vendors and the access they have to your data. Put safety measures in place to protect yourself and your customer information. A breech could, literally, put you out of business! As an example (more common than you think), if your medical practice allowed a breach of your patient's personal information and it became public, how many patients would you lose? How many would sue you? How many new patients would consider your practice?

Before you answer, consider the power of social media. How many negative reviews would you receive on Google? How about Facebook? How about your own website? Those don't even consider all of the local group pages and word-of-mouth. For a medical practice, and most businesses, this spells "D-O-O-M"!

To a patient/consumer, if I can't trust you to protect my personal information, especially with credit cards, how can I can trust you at all?? Here I go again . . . Golden Rule! As my mentor-who-doesn't-know-he-is-my-mentor, Jamie Dimon (CEO of JP Morgan Chase) says – "Treat your customer like you would treat your grandmother!" Would you allow your grandmother's credit card number to possibly be exposed to hackers? Hecks no! Treat your customers in the same way. Protect them!

Another area of vendor management to consider is timing risk. Basically, they deliver what they say, when they say they're going to do it. This is where a Service Level Agreement (SLA) comes into play. For example, if you submit your order to them by 2PM EST, you will receive it within 48 hours. If not, there is some sort of penalty, perhaps financial in nature.

That sounds great and protective. However, what if you are counting on that SLA and your vendor fails? Now what? How does that impact your ability to deliver to customers?

One commonly-used stance is to build a cushion into your schedule to account for a slide from your vendors. For example, if your vendor SLA is for delivery within 2 days, you use 3 days in your production schedule to account for a possible 1-day slippage. If your vendor slips by 1 day (a 50% slip, by the way!), you can still deliver to your customers. If they deliver on time, you now have 24 hours of leeway in your production schedule. You might be able to reduce labor costs (overtime) or deliver urgent orders as a result. With experience from each vendor, you can become more confident and adjust your schedule accordingly.

That being said, don't hesitate to include performance clauses, specifically financial penalties, in your vendor agreements. In no way is this meant to be punitive towards your vendors.

If you never collect a financial penalty, that would be optimal.

After all, you don't *want* them to break the terms of the SLA, right? That just jams up your process and causes you to scramble to meet your obligations. That is far less than optimal for you!

Contrarily, the purpose of the financial penalties is to incent vendors to meet the terms of your agreement. How is that? Won't they be irritated with penalties? Well, truth be told, they might not be happy with them. However, if you communicate your reasoning for wanting to include them, that usually alleviates the tension. They are also business owners.

This works exactly as it does with late payment penalties on invoices. You actually don't want to collect money for this! You just want your vendor to perform per your SLA. However, consider this scenario – your vendor has a production issue and it isn't possible for them to meet every customer SLA. How do they prioritize production in that case? Which customer receives their order and which is forced to wait?

If your vendor will incur a financial penalty for not meeting your SLA, but not for your competitor . . . you will get your order in a timely manner and your competitor will not. That is purely a financial decision on their part (and maybe they like you a little more too ☺). Think about it – what would you do? Delivering late to Customer A (you) will cost them a $200 financial penalty; delivering late to Customer B won't cost them anything. THIS is the advantage that including financial penalties in your SLA gains you.

OK, what else?

If it makes financial sense and is available, you can consider consolidating more business with one vendor. That will give you additional leverage to negotiate more preferential terms with them. Under that guise, be aware of all products each of your vendors provide.

That could open incremental opportunities for you

Of course, don't compromise anything that will impact your employees or customers. In the former, perhaps a cheaper, but inferior, product causes unnecessary frustration on the production line, which increases production cost. With the latter, the decreased quality negatively impacts your customers. Neither of those scenarios are worth considering.

If, in fact, you are able to take advantage of additional volume (and discount) from a particular vendor, I do have a word of caution: you **have** to mindful of vendor concentration risk. I cover this more extensively in Chapter 10. Be sure to check that out so you don't expose your business to undue risk.

The net message is to always have a Plan B. That goes for dang-near everything, but especially with vendors. Plan B's are most critical where you have little or no control, and that is applicable with vendors. You have no control whatsoever over any situation they might encounter in their business. Therefore, your risk with them is probably higher than any risk you have under your own roof. Make sure you account for it accordingly.

Certainly, contracts or agreements provide some peace of mind but, at the end of the day, if your vendor experiences a catastrophic situation, that all goes out the window. At that point, they are in survival mode and they will make their decisions accordingly – buddy, contract or not. Survival is the **THE** most influential frame of mind there is. It trumps everything! As you well know, a business owner most readily recognizes the impact on them, their family and their employees. In that situation, their decisions will likely follow that hierarchy.

Notice you and your company are nowhere in that decision hierarchy. Now, hopefully your vendors will never be faced with that scenario. But, as you know, it is the nature of the beast and you need to prepare yourself for it to some extent. Unfortunately, it happens and it might happen to a vendor upon whom you rely.

I have a client who has an accountant that does their tax & bookkeeping services. Once I reviewed a copy of their contract, I came to find that some of the things they were paying me to do were supposed to be done by their accountant! However, get this, they had not been done for almost two years! My client had been paying for something they weren't getting for about two years. Without realizing it, they began to pay *me* to do these tasks because they recognized it was something they needed. Put another way – part of what they were paying me to do was a complete waste of their money. They were already paying for it with their accountant!

This is where annual contract review comes into play

Look, I get it – you might have a bunch of contracts with several vendors. But look at it this way – if you thought your cell phone bill covered unlimited data, but in a certain month, they charged you $100 extra for data overage, what would you do? Would you just pay the bill? Or, would you investigate why you were being charged extra? I'm hoping you chose the latter.

No matter how much revenue and how big your business gets, you need to have the same diligence. Of course, your tolerance level is different for a $10 million business vs. a $100k business. As you grow, it isn't worth your time to investigate every potential $5 over-charge. However, by the same token, you can afford to pay someone else to worry about those lesser charges. Never get into the situation of blindly paying invoices. I don't care how big your company is, that is a dangerous place to be. Someone has to be watching the purse strings, even if it isn't you.

That is an example of where they signed the contract several years ago but nobody is paying attention to the details of the contract. Don't get there. As things varied along the way and some people came and some people went, the firm started to get a little soft and they stopped doing some things and my client didn't realize it. An annual review would have brought this to light much sooner as well as saved them time and money!

Here is a simple one that in the "busy-ness" of everything can get overlooked . . . open communication is critical. Make sure you have multiple points of contact.

I had a situation with a client that experienced a late delivery from a vendor. I had just started with this client and it was raw material they needed to complete customer orders. They called the salesperson but he was on vacation. They literally had no one else in the company who could deal with this issue. So, of course I said, "Let's just look at their website." Well, the company didn't have a website. Then, we looked for a phone number, only to find there was none?! Point being, make sure you have *multiple* points of contact so you can avoid that type of situation.

You want to make sure you do an in-depth contract review *before* you sign anything. I'll give one quick example: I walked into a client that had a 5-year contract. They hadn't really read the small print stating the contract extended automatically. In the meantime, we determined it wasn't a good contract. We said, "OK, we're going to drop this thing." Well, unfortunately, they were already stuck in it for an additional two years. I suggested "Plan C" – let's exit the contract. What's the exit clause? As you can guess, the exit clause was cost prohibitive so we were stuck with it for those extra two years. Ugh.

Read the contract details. If need be, get a professional opinion to cover yourself. The money spent will be well worth it.

Last, but not least, how to get vendors to fight over your business? Here's a quick story to illustrate it . . .

With a small manufacturing company, we had a particular product that was our largest expense on the raw material side. I spoke with three vendors that have the exact same product with exactly the same delivery SLAs. I invited them in for a meeting with me to bid on a contract with us. This is where it gets interesting . . .

I had them all come in at around the same time. Gosh darn it – what a scheduling mishap! ☺ Of course, they all know each other because they are competitors in the industry.

Cutting to the chase, guess what happened? They quickly determined what was going down & they knew their bid had to be super-competitive to earn the business. That made my job as easy as pie! No hard sell; no arm-twisting.

Once I received all bids, because I am a loyalty guy & as I had disclosed to all of the bidders (to further ramp-up the competition), I did go back to our current vendor to give them the opportunity to match the lowest price. Of course, I gave them a timely deadline so we could quickly wrap things up & start saving money! Although their initial bid had not done so, they chose to slightly beat the price of our lowest bidder in order to keep our business.

This one simple technique required minimal effort, yet saved us tens of thousands of dollars! It didn't cost us anything but saved us a bunch of money. It was as simple as that.

Don't overlook "simple"! Too often we over-complicate things & miss opportunities right under our nose.

Chapter 10

MANAGING RISKS YOU CANNOT AFFORD TO IGNORE

While this might not be the sexiest business topic to discuss, it is critical to your ongoing success. In this chapter we are going to talk about risk management – specifically, external risk management. We will tackle internal risk management in volume II of this book. We'll talk through some essential guidelines that will provide the tools you'll need to set up a risk management plan or to strengthen the one you already have in place.

We're going to start by talking through risk associated with competitors. You will always have new competitors that will join the fold.

- Are they local competitors?
- Are they outside of your general area?

Don't hesitate to secret shop them and check out *their* website.

Review your existing competitors. Have they changed anything significantly – pricing, marketing, scale, etc.? How would it impact you if one of your local competitors recently closed? What would an economic downturn mean for them? What it *could* mean for you, hopefully, is an opportunity, and not necessarily a risk. For example, you could decide to step-up your marketing efforts to fill that gap and capture additional market share.

Presuming you already have a marketing plan in place, the cost to pick-up the slack and scoop up business from one that has closed will usually only pose minimal risk. You may need to increase your inventory to be ready for the additional volume. There is risk there if you don't sell it or you over-buy inventory and end up having waste. However, more positively, you can turn a risk into an opportunity, which is obviously a good situation.

Know this:
If you don't seize the opportunity, someone else will!

Another external risk to consider is market changes. There's a whole litany of things that encompass market changes. One of the things that sticks out initially, is material costs. For example, if you produce widgets that require manufacturing. Raw material costs are obviously something out of your control but something critical to keep your eye on.

Is it just that your supplier has increased their costs to you? If so, you can shop around to see if you can find a better deal. Along those lines, make sure you're looking at all your primary suppliers and reviewing your contracts with them at least annually or as things materially change in your business. You want to make sure your costs are staying in the current market rate range so you're not at a pricing disadvantage vs. your competition. In addition, if your business is growing and, therefore, so is your volume, you want to talk to them about price breaks at certain volume intervals. These two items alone are a big reason why, in most cases, I suggest not signing anything longer than a 1-year commitment with any supplier. In fact, in most scenarios you want to commit to the shortest possible timeframe to provide you the future flexibility you need.

A couple additional things I'll mention on market changes where the risks aren't always so obvious. There's a ton of them, of course, but the ones I want to point out are things that aren't as obvious – like transportation issues. What do I mean by that?

There are several different ways you can approach this but here are a few examples:

Do your suppliers get most of their materials from the rail system? Maybe there's a strike; maybe there's a significant chunk of the rail system that is down for some reason. Is that going to impact their ability to get what they need to produce the goods, to get them to you for what you need? If so, this may result in temporary price increases for raw materials.

Likewise, you know that it *could* be a lot of different things. There could be a pilot strike and perhaps you get a lot of your goods from your suppliers via air transportation. Things like that may affect you in the short or long-term, but it's important for you to stay on top of things and know why you are experiencing a cost increase. Also, as much as possible, stay proactively in front of these issues so you can project impacts. That way you can steer around stumbling blocks or at least lessen their impact.

Always have a Plan B!

On the flip side, it can also hurt you directly, depending how *you* get *your* goods out to the market. If you have situations where, let's say DHL, UPS or FedEx have a contract with you, and one of them has a worker's strike. How is that going to impact *you* (and your customers) if you have all of your eggs in one basket? You're likely not ready for that, but it could *really* have a significant downstream impact on your business via the people that you're sending your products to... customers or distributors.

They don't want to hear about strikes, just like you wouldn't; they just want their stuff. They would likely look at that as *your* problem to solve. You need to figure out something in advance, as a plan B, so that those expecting product from you don't even know there was ever a problem. This is yet another way to set yourself apart from your competitors because many of them will **not** have a Plan B. They will have a laundry list of excuses to their customers. A big part of risk management is mitigating the risk as much as possible, so that's something that's very important to address in advance.

The last thing I'll mention about market changes, which again, is not necessarily something that is obvious, is... the weather and natural disasters. One of the things that's rarely considered. I had a client that had this situation happen to them. That's why it's always in the front of my mind.

If you have a supplier, for example, that is based in, let's say, Florida. Everyone knows there's a hurricane season every year. Well, what would that mean to your supplier if there was a significant hurricane, which again, could impact transportation or their plant, directly. If it's a significant event, maybe they've lost their workers for a while, things like that happen.

If you have that ONE way to mitigate, something you prepared for in advance, you may be able to work around it. However, to do this, it may lead into whether you can afford it. If your balance sheet and cash flow situation permit, you could stock up on materials from that particular supplier during hurricane season. Then you can make sure you can literally *and* figuratively "weather the storm" in situations like that. Again, your competitors are likely not employing risk mitigation in this manner so you will look like a superstar to your customers.

This is something that's not obvious but is very necessary to prepare for because, let me tell you, if it hits you, you're going to know it! If you are caught off guard, it's not going to be a good situation. As I mentioned, I went through this unfortunate situation with one of my clients. I had just started working with him about two months earlier. He had not considered or prepared for this type of risk. In order to fulfill orders timely, we had to scramble to find an alternate supplier. Of course, because we had not previously developed that relationship and it was a rush order, we paid handsomely for that lack of risk management. The good news is, we did figure it out and were able to fulfill orders and keep our customers happy. Needless to say, we put new steps in place to mitigate that risk for the future.

Let's shift gears a bit – to managing external risk in regards to customers. Let's dig right into this – this seems to be a prevalent issue with small businesses . . . having too much concentration with only one, or just a few customers. For example, you might have <u>ONE</u> client that is 80% of your annual revenue... one customer = 80%! Now imagine for a second:

- What would happen if that particular customer takes their business elsewhere?

- What if their new purchasing manager has a buddy that works at a competitor?

- What if they have overall financial issues and drop their order volume?

- Maybe their business is on a downswing due to external economic factors?

- Maybe they lost a key salesperson and *they* have a 30% drop in their sales?

- Maybe they've just decided to cut corners and now they're ordering 20% less from you?

What does all of that mean? Is your business at risk? Of course, it is! Many of the aforementioned factors are completely out of your control. Yet if that customer is 80% of your revenue, it could have a significant detrimental impact on your business.

Let's illustrate this with numbers to paint a clearer picture of what that could look like:

Your annual sales	$500,000
Sales from customer ABC	400,000 [if 80%]
Customer ABC drops 50%	-200,000 [50% of $400k]

Your new annual sales: $300,000 [presuming all else equal]

Your sales just dropped by 40% because you lost 50% from one customer! OUCH!

What would that mean for your company? What drastic measures would you need to take? How many people would you need to layoff? Could your company survive that big of a hit?

There are a few ways to mitigate customer concentration risk. The first of which, of course, is to continue growing your business with new customers. I know – easier said than done. In the meantime, this probably sounds counterintuitive but you should strongly consider not taking additional business from that customer. Of course, every situation is different but it should definitely be a consideration. Alternatively, you may have heard this one before . . . ensure you have a Plan B in the event any of the above scenarios occur. That could be in the form of a line-of-credit you could tap into, if needed, for example.

You could also add some contract terms with that customer but you've got to make it a win-win. That could possibly protect you a little bit in a negative scenario. Contract terms could be certain minimum volume thresholds from them in exchange for better pricing for them. You may still be down, but not as significantly as you would be otherwise. That's another way lessen the impact of that concentration risk. However, always keep in mind – in extreme circumstances, even those contract stipulations won't help you. If their backs are against the wall, they may have no other choice but to break the contract terms in order for them to stay in business. Or, worse yet, they might need to file bankruptcy.

The customer concentration risk lends itself to doing diligence on your larger customers. That should be a foregone conclusion for every business. You should be doing that long before you would allow any one customer to be a big piece of your revenue base.

Another not-so-obvious external risk is when your customer base itself is changing. Let me give you one quick example – I worked with a family-owned standalone jewelry store that had been in the same location for many years. Their customer base was continuing to age but they did not change with the times and go with the natural flow of things.

This problem was two-fold:

1) They weren't bringing in new, younger customers

2) They were still marketing in the same way they had in the past. Because of their stellar reputation, they were able to heavily rely on word-of-mouth. However, as I mentioned, their existing customer base had aged a fair amount.

They just continued to ride their existing customers, which is fine in some ways because they are part of your base and they are loyal. However, as those customers aged, they were buying less jewelry.

Think about the typical sales life cycle of a jewelry buyer: getting married in their 20s-30s; buying spouse jewelry gifts in their 40s-50s, maybe a little into their 60s; once they are into their 70s-80s, how much jewelry do they usually purchase? Their local customer base is quite affluent so it served them well over the years. However, the area had not seen a much of a turnover of older people moving out to make way for younger affluent people.

The combination of these two occurrences led them to call me as their revenue continued shrinking. Much of it was due to working in the weeds and not thinking in a more strategic manner. They did not appropriately manage the mix of their customer base. They had all of their eggs in one segment of their possible customer base. They suffered from a different form of concentration risk.

Two additional external risks I want to mention in this chapter are *suppliers* and *cyber risk*. The latter is a constantly evolving topic that could be an entire book by itself but I will touch on it a bit here.

Supplier/vendor concentration risk is similar to what we discussed with customer concentration risk so I won't spend too much time on it. If you have one raw material that's a significant part of your process, you can be caught off guard by what your supplier experiences. It would be completely out of your control. Things such as:

1) Worker strike

2) Facility damage – fire, flood, etc.

3) Natural disaster

4) Worker shortage

5) Transportation challenges

6) Financial problems

This list is eerily similar to the customer concentration list a few pages back, isn't it?

As with customer concentration risk, you've *got* to make sure you're not too concentrated and, repeat after me . . .

Always, always, always, have a plan B!

If you're stuck with a supplier that can't get you what you need for production, that means you can't service **your** customers! And then, inevitably, it negatively impacts *your* business in the downstream. The impact of that can be significant to your company.

The final piece of external risk I'll mention is cyber risk. As I alluded to earlier, since this topic is continually growing and evolving, we could probably devote an entire book to it! Primarily, if you process financial transactions or house any type of confidential information online, do not "cheap-out" or ignore cyber risk. Doing so, has the potential to put you out of business with just one compromised situation. In fact:

60% of small businesses go out of business after a data breach[19]

---

[19] https://www.mvpworks.com/images/EBooks/Cybersecurity-tips-for-Medical-Practices.pdf

Look at it this way – if it can happen to Fortune 500 companies, like we regularly see in news headlines, it can certainly happen to you. That's a great segue way

I mentioned paying particular to this if you have confidential information online – like a medical practice. While working with a medical practice, I was doing some research and found this quite interesting:

53% of all cyber security breaches are healthcare-related[20]
(more than double than any other industry)

The reason being: healthcare providers are expected to have deep pockets (to possibly pay "ransom" for stolen information). Unfortunately, if they're a small practice, it's likely they're slow to upgrade to current security measures.

Another related interesting fact:

On the dark web, medical records are worth as much as $60 per record vs. only $1-$3 for the much more commonly publicized credit card number theft[21]. Hackers know it is much easier to cancel a credit card than to change your social security number.

Clearly, there is much more bang-for-the-buck for cyber thieves to obtain medical records. Combine that with the earlier-mentioned presumed deep pockets and slow adoption of current security measures and it begins to make sense.

---

[20] https://www.thedoctors.com/articles/cybersecurity-insurance-for-medical-practices-the-basics/
[21] https://www.fastcompany.com/3061543/on-the-dark-web-medical-records-are-a-hot-commodity

What it boils down to – if you process financial transactions or house confidential information online, hire a professional to help you stay at the forefront of the ever-changing technology. Also, I would suggest speaking with an insurance professional to consider covering yourself in that way as well.

CLOSING

Do you have a whole slew of new ideas to increase your profits? If not, this book is a failure. If so, I am a happy author.

Congratulations! You made it through all of volume I of "Pathway to Profits"! Wait, what? There's more? No one told me about any of that noise! Yeah, tell me about it – I'm with ya!

As you may have gathered by now, there will be a volume II of this book. Even saying that is a bit crazy. Before I wrote my first book, "How to Be a Cash Flow Pro: A Mr. Biz Guide to Business Owner Insomnia", I had absolutely 0% intention of ever writing even a single book, let alone multiple books.

Seriously, if you knew how torturous it is for me to write, you would never think I would be finishing a 2nd book, with plans for a 3rd. Well, my immediate family might believe it because they get to hear me complain/whine like a wimp about the writing process on the regular – DOH!

Let me do videos or speaking engagements all day-every day and I will be a Happy Camper.

Writing . . . not so much.

All right, enough about my love-hate relationship with writing books. I sincerely hope this book was helpful for you. If it was (or wasn't), don't hesitate to let me know at Ken@MrBizSolutions.com.

I would love to hear your feedback. If you send feedback in time, I will include it in volume II - "Pathway to <u>More</u> Profits". That book will be released in early 2020. However, if I have anything to say about it, that release date will be . . . Febru-never 34th, 20712 ☺ Just kidding.

Thank you for reading volume I! I do sincerely hope you found value with the content.

The most important aspect is to **take action**! Use the content to help optimize your company. Don't be paralyzed by inaction. As a Mr. Biz Weekly Tip says –

The road is riddled with flat squirrels that couldn't make a decision

Make a decision and take action, even if it ends up being wrong. You can always switch directions, if necessary. At least you will know there is no cheese down *that* tunnel. Use the data, create a new tunnel & charge down that one! It might take tunnel trip & it might take 10! I promise if you keep moving forward, you <u>**WILL**</u> get there! As a great man, Martin Luther King, Jr., once said:

"If you can't fly, then run;
if you can't run, then walk;
if you can't walk, then crawl;

but whatever you do, you have to keep moving
forward."

Please heed his wise words & TAKE ACTION! I promise you
will not regret it. That's precisely how you learn, adapt & try
again.

Without action you are stuck on the sidelines wondering or
wishing what would have/could have been a success. As Gary
Vee (Vaynerchuk) says:

"Ideas are sh*t! Execution is the game!"

OK – off my soapbox again . . .

To give you an idea of what will be included in volume II, here
is a brief rundown of the topics we will cover (in no particular
order):

- Invoicing changes to help you get paid faster

- Pricing for maximal profits. If your pricing is inaccurate,
  your business is digging its own grave. The more sales
  you generate, the deeper hole you dig!

- When is the right time & how to most optimally expand
  your business?

- How to retain your best employees

- Saving on expenses without hurting your business

- Small business basics you need to know to save money on your taxes

- What internal risks can cost you BIG TIME?!

- Measuring & monitoring to ensure optimal cash flow

- Incenting your employees for maximum loyalty

- 50 small business marketing tips you can implement today!

At the end of 20 chapters (both volumes combined), you will be a more profitable & more efficient business owner. That is the end goal.

Don't hesitate to connect with me on social media for helpful weekly free content for small business owners:

Facebook	Mr. Biz Solutions
Instagram	@MrBizSolutions
LinkedIn	Ken "Mr. Biz" Wentworth
Twitter	@MrBizTweets
Website	www.MrBizSolutions.com

If you are a business owner, I already have immense respect for you! Please, please stay connected - don't try to do it alone.

ABOUT THE AUTHOR

Ken "Mr. Biz" Wentworth is a strategic business partner who works with small business owners to help them operate more profitably and more efficiently.

His first book, "How to Be a Cash Flow Pro: A Mr. Biz Guide to Crushing Business Owner Insomnia" was an Amazon best-seller. He wrote that book to help the 82% of small business owners that fail due to cash flow challenges.

During his corporate career, Ken developed a diverse skillset by working in many different roles – Accountant, Investment Analyst, Operations Manager, Planning & Analysis Director and CFO for several different businesses. Academically, he has earned a BA in Accounting and an Honors Master's Degree in Financial Management.

Mr. Biz regularly speaks to professional organizations, hosts "B2B Radio" and founded Mr. Biz Solutions, an exclusive website created specifically to provide affordable business expertise for small business owners.

When your business has challenges, Mr. Biz has your solutions!

He is often quoted and appears as an expert on small business topics in a variety of publications as well as radio/podcast programs.

Philanthropically, Mr. Biz is involved with several charities. Primarily, he is Treasurer for his local Family Promise and is a featured member of the "Real Men Wear Pink" campaign of Columbus to help lead the fight against breast cancer.

Mr. Biz resides in the USA - Ohio with his wife and 3 children. Learn more at www.MrBizSolutions.com